# Company's Coming ®

# Greatest Hits

## Soups & Salads

www.**companys**coming.com
visit our web-site

**Over 175 best-selling recipes**

GREATEST HITS SERIES

# Soups & Salads

First printing April 2000

Canadian Cataloguing in Publication Data
Paré, Jean
    Greatest hits: soups & salads

Issued also in French under title: Jean Paré grands succès : soupes et salades.
(Greatest hits series)
Includes index.
ISBN 1-896891-35-7

    1. Soups. 2. Salads. I. Title. II. Title: Soups & salads. III. Series.

TX757.P37 2000     641.8'13     C00-900048-8

Published simultaneously in Canada
and the United States of America by
The Recipe Factory Inc. in conjunction with
Company's Coming Publishing Limited
2311 - 96 Street, Edmonton, Alberta,
Canada  T6N 1G3
Tel: 780 • 450-6223        Fax: 780 • 450-1857
www.companyscoming.com

Company's Coming is a registered trademark owned by Company's Coming Publishing Limited
Printed in Canada

FRONT COVER:
1. Tortellini In Broth, page 110
2. Marinated Vegetable Salad, page 60
3. Split Pea Soup, page 113
4. Fruit Salad, page 15

Props Courtesy Of:  Stokes, The Bay, X/S Wares

**www.companyscoming.com**
visit our web-site

# table of contents

# our cookbooks

## COMPANY'S COMING SERIES

150 Delicious Squares
Appetizers
Breads
Breakfasts & Brunches
Cakes
Casseroles
Chicken, Etc.
Cookies
Cooking for Two
Desserts
Dinners of the World
Fish & Seafood
Holiday Entertaining
Kids Cooking
Light Casseroles
Light Recipes
Lunches
Main Courses
Meatless Cooking
Microwave Cooking
Muffins & More
One-Dish Meals
Pasta
Pies
Pizza!
Preserves
Salads
Slow Cooker Recipes
Soups & Sandwiches
Starters
Stir-Fry - **NEW**
Vegetables

## ASSORTED TITLES

Beef Today!
Easy Entertaining
Kids Lunches

## GREATEST HITS

Biscuits, Muffins & Loaves
Dips, Spreads & Dressings
Sandwiches & Wraps - **NEW**
Soups & Salads - **NEW**

## LIFESTYLE SERIES

Grilling - **NEW**
Low-fat Cooking
Low-fat Pasta

## SELECT SERIES

30-Minute Meals
Beans & Rice
Ground Beef
Make-Ahead Salads
No-Bake Desserts
Sauces & Marinades

# company's coming story

Jean Paré grew up understanding that the combination of family, friends and home cooking is the essence of a good life. From her mother she learned to appreciate good cooking, while her father praised even her earliest attempts. When she left home she took with her many acquired family recipes, a love of cooking and an intriguing desire to read recipe books like novels!

In 1963, when her four children had all reached school age, Jean volunteered to cater the 50th anniversary of the Vermilion School of Agriculture, now Lakeland College. Working out of her home, Jean prepared a dinner for over 1000 people which launched a flourishing catering operation that continued for over eighteen years. During that time she was provided with countless opportunities to test new ideas with immediate feedback—resulting in empty plates and contented customers! Whether preparing cocktail sandwiches for a house party or serving a hot meal for 1500 people, Jean Paré earned a reputation for good food, courteous service and reasonable prices.

"Why don't you write a cookbook?" Time and again, as requests for her recipes mounted, Jean was asked that question. Jean's response was to team up with her son, Grant Lovig, in the fall of 1980 to form Company's Coming Publishing Limited. April 14, 1981, marked the debut of "150 DELICIOUS SQUARES", the first Company's Coming cookbook in what soon would become Canada's most popular cookbook series.

Jean Paré's operation has grown steadily from the early days of working out of a spare bedroom in her home. Full-time staff includes marketing personnel located in major cities across Canada. Home Office is based in Edmonton, Alberta in a modern building constructed specially for the company.

Today the company distributes throughout Canada and the United States in addition to numerous overseas markets, all under the guidance of Jean's daughter, Gail Lovig. Best-sellers many times over, Company's Coming cookbooks are published in English and French, plus a Spanish-language edition is available in Mexico. Familiar and trusted in home kitchens the world over, Company's Coming cookbooks are offered in a variety of formats, including the original softcover series.

Jean Paré's approach to cooking has always called for quick and easy recipes using everyday ingredients. Even when traveling, she is constantly on the lookout for new ideas to share with her readers. At home, she can usually be found researching and writing recipes, or working in the company's test kitchen. Jean continues to gain new supporters by adhering to what she calls "the golden rule of cooking": never share a recipe you wouldn't use yourself. It's an approach that works—*millions of times over!*

# foreword

The age-old restaurant question is, "Would you like soup or salad with your meal?" But we often ask the same question at home too. "Should I serve soup or salad with tonight's meal?" *Soups & Salads* has the answer to the question. In fact, it provides over 175 answers!

Soups have provided a warm beginning to many wintery night suppers for centuries. The number of ways to combine diced vegetables, chunks of meat and rich broths is almost endless. There's Meatball Soup, Chicken Curry Soup or Herbed Tomato Soup. And it doesn't stop there. Add pasta, rice or beans and you almost have a full meal. Try Zuppa Fagioli, Garbanzo Soup or Chicken Rice Soup with a basket of rolls and you're set for lunch. Soups can be clear broths such as Egg Flower Soup or creamy like Corn Chowder; vegetables can be the basis as in Asparagus Leek Soup or seafood offers us such possibilities as Shrimp And Mushroom Soup. Soups start your meal with just the right touch.

If your choice of a great beginning is a salad, then again, you're in luck. *Soups & Salads* is a collection of our most popular salads, and dressings to go with them. Toss Green Goddess Salad or mold Cucumber Mousse. Make a salad with pasta such as Oriental Pasta Salad or make it with rice such as Shrimpy Rice Salad. Serve pretty Coconut Marshmallow Salad or showy Super Salad. Or make a whole meal of Ginger Chicken Salad or Beef And Spinach Salad.

Keep *Soups & Salads* handy. You'll be picking and choosing one of these delicious recipes almost daily!

## each recipe

has been analyzed using the most updated version of the Canadian Nutrient File from Health Canada, which is based upon the United States Department of Agriculture (USDA) Nutrient Data Base.

Margaret Ng, B.Sc. (Hon), M.A.
Registered Dietician

# Salad Dressings

*I*t's amazing that a simple concoction of oil, vinegar and spices can bring so much life to a salad. From this basic recipe arise some interesting variations, such as those found in this section. With a few of these dressings on hand in your refrigerator, a salad can be made at a moment's notice. Some of these recipes such as House Dressing, page 9, also work well as a dip for vegetables, chips or crackers.

## ITALIAN DRESSING

*Great for marinating vegetables as well as greens.*

| | | |
|---|---|---|
| Cooking oil | 1 cup | 250 mL |
| Lemon juice | ¼ cup | 60 mL |
| White vinegar | ¼ cup | 60 mL |
| Granulated sugar | 2 tsp. | 10 mL |
| Salt | 1 tsp. | 5 mL |
| Dry mustard | ½ tsp. | 2 mL |
| Onion powder | ½ tsp. | 2 mL |
| Paprika | ½ tsp. | 2 mL |
| Dried whole oregano | ½ tsp. | 2 mL |
| Garlic powder (or 1 clove, crushed) | ½ tsp. | 2 mL |
| Ground thyme | ⅛ tsp. | 0.5 mL |

Measure all 11 ingredients into jar. Cover. Shake well. Chill for 2 hours. Makes 1½ cups (375 mL).

*1 tbsp. (15 mL): 84 Calories; 9.2 g Total Fat; 163 mg Sodium; trace Protein; 1 g Carbohydrate; trace Dietary Fiber*

## SUNNY DRESSING

*So smooth and special drizzled over a fresh fruit salad.*

| | | |
|---|---|---|
| Cream cheese, softened | 8 oz. | 250 g |
| Prepared orange juice | ¼ cup | 60 mL |
| Granulated sugar | ¼ cup | 60 mL |

Beat all 3 ingredients in small bowl until creamy. Makes about 1⅓ cups (325 mL).

*1 tbsp. (15 mL): 50 Calories; 4 g Total Fat; 34 mg Sodium; 1 g Protein; 3 g Carbohydrate; trace Dietary Fiber*

# CROUTONS

*Toss in with your favorite salad or drop a spoonful into a bowl of hot soup.*

| | | |
|---|---|---|
| **Day-old bread slices** | **8** | **8** |
| **Margarine, softened** | **½ cup** | **125 mL** |

Spread both sides of bread slices lightly with margarine. Stack slices 2 or 4 high. Cut into ½ inch (12 mm) cubes. Arrange on ungreased baking sheet. Bake in 300°F (150°C) oven for 25 to 30 minutes until golden brown. Stir occasionally while browning. If you prefer, stir-fry in frying pan until browned. Makes about 4 cups (1 L).

*¼ cup (60 mL): 92 Calories; 6.6 g Total Fat; 143 mg Sodium; 1 g Protein; 7 g Carbohydrate; trace Dietary Fiber*

**GARLIC CROUTONS:** Mix ½ tsp. (2 mL) garlic salt with margarine before buttering bread.

**HERB CROUTONS:** Mix ¼ tsp. (1 mL) each of garlic powder, dried whole oregano, dried thyme and dried sweet basil with margarine before buttering bread.

**PARMESAN CROUTONS:** Sprinkle both sides of buttered bread with grated Parmesan cheese.

**SEASONED CROUTONS:** Mix ½ tsp. (2 mL) seasoned salt with margarine before buttering bread.

# TOMATO RELISH DRESSING

*This will remind you of a well-known commercial salad dressing.*

| | | |
|---|---|---|
| **Margarine** | **¼ cup** | **60 mL** |
| **All-purpose flour** | **¼ cup** | **60 mL** |
| **Water** | **1 cup** | **250 mL** |
| **Ketchup** | **1 cup** | **250 mL** |
| **White vinegar** | **½ cup** | **125 mL** |
| **Granulated sugar** | **1 cup** | **250 mL** |
| **Celery salt** | **1 tsp.** | **5 mL** |
| **Onion powder** | **1 tsp.** | **5 mL** |
| **Salt** | **1 tbsp.** | **15 mL** |
| **Pepper** | **½ tsp.** | **2 mL** |
| **Sweet pickle relish** | **½ cup** | **125 mL** |

Melt margarine in medium saucepan. Add flour. Mix.

Stir in water, ketchup and vinegar until boiling and thickened.

Add remaining 6 ingredients. Stir until sugar is dissolved. Makes 4 cups (1 L).

*1 tbsp. (15 mL): 27 Calories; 1.5 g Total Fat; 421 mg Sodium; trace Protein; 10 g Carbohydrate; trace Dietary Fiber*

**Variation:** For a less sweet dressing omit ketchup. Add 1 can (5½ oz., 156 mL) tomato paste.

*The easiest way to make bread cubes is to first freeze the bread, then trim and cube a stack of frozen slices.*

# HOUSE DRESSING

*Good over any salad. Also makes a good vegetable dip.*

| | | |
|---|---|---|
| Light salad dressing (or mayonnaise) | 1 cup | 250 mL |
| Ketchup | ½ cup | 125 mL |
| White vinegar | 2 tbsp. | 30 mL |
| Granulated sugar | 2 tbsp. | 30 mL |
| Milk | 2 tbsp. | 30 mL |
| Salt | ½ tsp. | 2 mL |
| Prepared horseradish | ½ tsp. | 2 mL |
| Worcestershire sauce | ¼ tsp. | 1 mL |

Stir salad dressing and ketchup together in small bowl.

Mix in remaining 6 ingredients in order given. Stir well until sugar and salt are dissolved. Makes about 1¾ cups (425 mL).

*1 tbsp. (15 mL):* 34 Calories; 2.2 g Total Fat; 182 mg Sodium; trace Protein; 4 g Carbohydrate; trace Dietary Fiber

# CREAMY GARLIC DRESSING

*Dress a salad with this for a creamy flavor boost.*

| | | |
|---|---|---|
| Light salad dressing (or mayonnaise) | ½ cup | 125 mL |
| Milk | ¼ cup | 60 mL |
| White vinegar | 2 tsp. | 10 mL |
| Garlic powder | 1 tsp. | 5 mL |
| Dry mustard | ¼ tsp. | 1 mL |
| Granulated sugar | ½ tsp. | 2 mL |
| Onion powder | ⅛ tsp. | 0.5 mL |
| Salt | ⅛ tsp. | 0.5 mL |
| Pepper | 1/16 tsp. | 0.5 mL |

Combine all 9 ingredients in small bowl. Stir well. Makes a generous ¾ cup (175 mL).

*1 tbsp. (15 mL):* 33 Calories; 2.6 g Total Fat; 108 mg Sodium; trace Protein; 2 g Carbohydrate; trace Dietary Fiber

# COOKED SALAD DRESSING

*A recipe from a way, way back. This has a real zip to it so use only a little to begin with.*

| | | |
|---|---|---|
| Granulated sugar | ½ cup | 125 mL |
| All-purpose flour | 2 tbsp. | 30 mL |
| Dry mustard | 1 tbsp. | 15 mL |
| Salt | 1 tsp. | 5 mL |
| Large eggs | 3 | 3 |
| Milk | 1 cup | 250 mL |
| White vinegar | ½ cup | 125 mL |
| Water | ½ cup | 125 mL |

Put sugar, flour, mustard and salt in top of double boiler. Stir until flour is mixed in well. Beat in eggs, 1 at a time.

Stir in milk, vinegar and water. Cook over boiling water, stirring often, until thickened. Pour into container. Cover. Chill. Makes about 2½ cups (625 mL).

*1 tbsp. (15 mL):* 21 Calories; 0.5 g Total Fat; 73 mg Sodium; 1 g Protein; 7 g Carbohydrate; trace Dietary Fiber

# Coleslaw Salads

*U*sually made from shredded cabbage, coleslaw gets its wonderful and distinctive flavors from the dressing and spices or herbs that have been included. Coleslaw is a traditional favorite at barbecues or buffet tables, but also makes a wonderful side dish at almost any meal. If you want to try something a little different, consider Special Coleslaw, page 13, with its unique flavor and color, or Sauerkraut Salad, page 11, which can also be used as a savory condiment for wieners or hamburgers.

## SEEDY SLAW

*Full of seeds and bean sprouts.*

| | | |
|---|---|---|
| Grated cabbage, lightly packed | 1 cup | 250 mL |
| Chopped green pepper | 1½ tbsp. | 25 mL |
| Sliced fresh mushrooms | ¼ cup | 60 mL |
| Fresh bean sprouts | 1 cup | 250 mL |
| Green onion, thinly sliced | 1 | 1 |
| **DRESSING** | | |
| Ground walnuts (or sunflower seeds) | 1½ tbsp. | 25 mL |
| Toasted sesame seeds (see Tip, page 21) | 1½ tbsp. | 25 mL |
| Cooking oil | 1½ tsp. | 7 mL |
| White vinegar | 1½ tsp. | 7 mL |
| Granulated sugar | 1 tsp. | 5 mL |
| Dry mustard, just a pinch | | |
| Water | 1½ tsp. | 7 mL |
| Worcestershire sauce | ⅛ tsp. | 0.5 mL |
| Chicken bouillon powder | ¼ tsp. | 1 mL |
| Salt | ⅛ tsp. | 0.5 mL |
| Pepper | 1/16 tsp. | 0.5 mL |

Combine first 5 ingredients in medium bowl. Stir.

**Dressing:** Mix all 11 ingredients in small bowl. Stir well. Add to cabbage mixture. Toss. Makes 1½ cups (375 mL), enough for 2 servings.

*1 serving: 136 Calories; 10.3 g Total Fat; 276 mg Sodium; 3 g Protein; 10 g Carbohydrate; 3 g Dietary Fiber*

# CURRY SLAW

*The mild touch of curry powder gives a delicious twist to this coleslaw.*

| | | |
|---|---|---|
| Grated cabbage, lightly packed | 3 cups | 750 mL |
| Medium carrot, grated | 1 | 1 |
| **DRESSING** | | |
| Light salad dressing (or mayonnaise) | ½ cup | 125 mL |
| Granulated sugar | 1½ tbsp. | 25 mL |
| White vinegar | 1 tbsp. | 15 mL |
| Onion flakes | 2 tsp. | 10 mL |
| Celery seed | ¼ tsp. | 1 mL |
| Prepared mustard | ¼ tsp. | 1 mL |
| Curry powder | ⅛ tsp. | 0.5 mL |

Combine cabbage and carrot in medium bowl. Chill until serving.

**Dressing:** Mix all 7 ingredients in small bowl. Chill until serving. Pour over salad just before serving. Stir well. Serves 4.

*1 serving: 137 Calories; 8.1 g Total Fat; 262 mg Sodium; 1 g Protein; 16 g Carbohydrate; 2 g Dietary Fiber*

# SAUERKRAUT SALAD

*Flavor is excellent and color is showy. Best when served the next day.*

| | | |
|---|---|---|
| Can of sauerkraut, drained | 28 oz. | 796 mL |
| Chopped celery | 1 cup | 250 mL |
| Chopped onion | ½ cup | 125 mL |
| Grated carrot | ½ cup | 125 mL |
| Chopped green or red pepper | ½ cup | 125 mL |
| Pimiento slivers | 2 tbsp. | 30 mL |
| Granulated sugar | 1 cup | 250 mL |
| White vinegar | ½ cup | 125 mL |

Combine first 6 ingredients in large bowl.

Heat sugar and vinegar in small saucepan, stirring occasionally, until boiling. Remove from heat. Cool to lukewarm. Pour over vegetables. Stir. Cover. Chill overnight. Makes 5 cups (1.25 L), enough for 10 servings.

*1 serving: 108 Calories; 0.2 g Total Fat; 381 mg Sodium; 1 g Protein; 27 g Carbohydrate; 3 g Dietary Fiber*

# CONFETTI COLESLAW

*Contains tomato and onion. Different from the usual slaw. Very good.*

| | | |
|---|---|---|
| Grated cabbage, lightly packed | 3 cups | 750 mL |
| Medium carrot, grated | 1 | 1 |
| Chopped green onion | 2 tbsp. | 30 mL |
| Medium tomato, chopped | 1 | 1 |
| **DRESSING** | | |
| Light salad dressing (or mayonnaise) | ½ cup | 125 mL |
| Milk | 2 tbsp. | 30 mL |
| Prepared mustard | ½ tsp. | 2 mL |
| Granulated sugar | 1 tsp. | 5 mL |
| Onion powder | ¼ tsp. | 1 mL |
| Celery seed | ¼ tsp. | 1 mL |
| Salt | ⅛ tsp. | 0.5 mL |

Combine first 4 ingredients in large bowl. Mix lightly. Chill.

**Dressing:** Mix all 7 ingredients in small bowl. Pour over salad. Toss together. Serves 4.

*1 serving: 128 Calories; 8.3 g Total Fat; 362 mg Sodium; 2 g Protein; 13 g Carbohydrate; 2 g Dietary Fiber*

## PASTA SLAW

*Also contains tuna and shrimp. A new spin on coleslaw.*

| | | |
|---|---|---|
| Small shell pasta | 1½ cups | 375 mL |
| Boiling water | 2 qts. | 2 L |
| Cooking oil (optional) | 2 tsp. | 10 mL |
| Salt | 1½ tsp. | 7 mL |
| Grated cabbage, lightly packed | 3 cups | 750 mL |
| Grated carrot | ½ cup | 125 mL |
| Thinly sliced celery | ½ cup | 125 mL |
| Chopped green onion | ½ cup | 125 mL |
| Canned solid white tuna, packed in water, drained and broken up | 6½ oz. | 184 g |
| **DRESSING** | | |
| Light salad dressing (or mayonnaise) | ½ cup | 125 mL |
| Milk | 2 tbsp. | 30 mL |
| White vinegar | 1 tsp. | 5 mL |
| Granulated sugar | ½ tsp. | 2 mL |
| Onion powder | ¼ tsp. | 1 mL |
| Celery salt | ⅛ tsp. | 0.5 mL |
| Cooked fresh (or frozen, thawed) small shrimp | ¼ lb. | 113 g |

Cook pasta in boiling water, cooking oil and salt in large uncovered pot or Dutch oven for 8 to 11 minutes, stirring occasionally, until tender but firm. Drain. Rinse with cold water. Drain well. Return pasta to pot.

Add cabbage, carrot, celery, green onion and tuna. Toss together.

**Dressing:** Measure first 6 ingredients into small bowl. Stir together. Pour over pasta mixture. Toss to coat. Divide among 6 individual salad plates or serve in large bowl.

Scatter shrimp over top. Serves 6.

*1 serving: 223 Calories; 6.6 g Total Fat; 348 mg Sodium; 14 g Protein; 26 g Carbohydrate; 2 g Dietary Fiber*

## COLESLAW

*Bright and colorful with creamy white dressing. Prepare vegetables in morning, or even the day before, and chill in airtight container until ready to add dressing.*

| | | |
|---|---|---|
| Shredded green cabbage, lightly packed | 6 cups | 1.5 L |
| Shredded red cabbage, lightly packed | ½ cup | 125 mL |
| Medium carrots, grated | 2 | 2 |
| Chopped green onion | ⅓ cup | 75 mL |
| **DRESSING** | | |
| Light sour cream | 1 cup | 250 mL |
| Light salad dressing (or mayonnaise) | 2 tbsp. | 30 mL |
| White vinegar | 1½ tbsp. | 25 mL |
| Celery seed | ⅛ tsp. | 0.5 mL |
| Salt | ½ tsp. | 2 mL |
| Pepper | ¼ tsp. | 1 mL |

Combine first 4 ingredients in large bowl. Stir.

**Dressing:** Mix all 6 ingredients in small bowl. Stir well. Makes 1⅓ cups (325 mL) dressing. Pour over cabbage mixture. Toss thoroughly. Makes 8 cups (2 L), enough for 16 servings.

*1 serving: 30 Calories; 1.6 g Total Fat; 113 mg Sodium; 1 g Protein; 3 g Carbohydrate; 1 g Dietary Fiber*

# SPECIAL COLESLAW

*This is a nice brunch or buffet salad. Bright, colorful and great taste.*

| Grated cabbage, lightly packed | 2 cups | 500 mL |
|---|---|---|
| Can of crushed pineapple, drained and 1 tbsp. (15 mL) juice reserved | 8 oz. | 227 mL |
| Miniature marshmallows | 50 | 50 |
| Slivered or sliced almonds (optional) | ½ cup | 125 mL |
| Medium coconut | ½ cup | 125 mL |
| Light salad dressing (or mayonnaise) | ½ cup | 125 mL |
| Reserved pineapple juice | | |
| Cayenne pepper, just a pinch | | |

Combine first 5 ingredients in large bowl.

Mix salad dressing, reserved pineapple juice and cayenne pepper in small bowl. Pour over salad. Mix well. Serves 6.

*1 serving:* 155 Calories; 10.5 g Total Fat; 173 mg Sodium; 3 g Protein; 16 g Carbohydrate; 1 g Dietary Fiber

# NOODLE SLAW

*A good way to doctor a store-bought salad.*

| Bag of shredded cabbage with carrot | 1 lb. | 454 g |
|---|---|---|
| Package instant noodles, chicken-flavored, broken up, seasoning packet reserved | 3 oz. | 85 g |

**DRESSING**

| Reserved seasoning packet | | |
|---|---|---|
| Soy sauce | 2 tbsp. | 30 mL |
| Cooking oil | 2 tsp. | 10 mL |
| Granulated sugar | 2 tsp. | 10 mL |
| Pepper | ¼ tsp. | 1 mL |
| Toasted sesame seeds (see Tip, page 21) | 4 tsp. | 20 mL |

Combine cabbage mixture and noodles in large bowl.

**Dressing:** Stir all 6 ingredients in small bowl. Pour over salad just before serving. Toss together well. Makes 7½ cups (1.8 L), enough for 7 generous servings.

*1 serving:* 87 Calories; 2.4 g Total Fat; 379 mg Sodium; 3 g Protein; 14 g Carbohydrate; 2 g Dietary Fiber

*Save time making coleslaw by using a package of shredded cabbage from the grocery store. Even better is the mixed shredded green cabbage, red cabbage and carrot.*

# Fruit Salads

fruit salad is a colorful medley of sweet flavors that can be served as a side dish to your main course, or as a healthy dessert. Try Melon Salad, page 19, as part of your next Sunday brunch, or Spinach Fruit Salad, page 16, when the warm summer weather begs something a little more luscious and cool.

## TUNA FRUIT SALAD

*So fruity mellow. You will think you're eating dessert.*

| | | |
|---|---|---|
| Can of pineapple chunks, drained and cut in half | 8 oz. | 227 mL |
| Large banana | 1 | 1 |
| Sliced or diced celery | ½ cup | 125 mL |
| Can of tuna, drained and flaked | 6½ oz. | 184 g |
| Light salad dressing (or mayonnaise) | 2 tbsp. | 30 mL |
| Sweet pickle relish | 2 tsp. | 10 mL |
| Milk | 1 tsp. | 5 mL |
| Salt | ¼ tsp. | 1 mL |
| Paprika | ¼ tsp. | 1 mL |
| Light salad dressing (or mayonnaise) | 3 tbsp. | 50 mL |
| Milk | 2 tsp. | 10 mL |
| Granulated sugar | ¼ tsp. | 1 mL |
| Shredded or torn lettuce, lightly packed | 4 cups | 1 L |

Combine pineapple, banana, celery and tuna in medium bowl. Toss lightly.

Mix first amount of salad dressing, relish, first amount of milk, salt and paprika in small bowl. Add to tuna mixture. Toss lightly.

Stir second amounts of salad dressing and milk and sugar together in large bowl.

Add lettuce. Toss. Divide among 4 salad plates or spread on large platter. Spoon tuna mixture over top. Serves 4.

*1 serving:* 167 Calories; 6.1 g Total Fat; 496 mg Sodium; 12 g Protein; 18 g Carbohydrate; 2 g Dietary Fiber

# FRUIT SALAD

*A very fresh and colorful salad.*

**DRESSING**

| | | |
|---|---|---|
| Avocado, peeled, pitted and mashed | 1 | 1 |
| Light salad dressing (or mayonnaise) | ²/₃ cup | 150 mL |
| Lemon juice | 1 tbsp. | 15 mL |
| Granulated sugar | 1 tbsp. | 15 mL |

**SALAD**

| | | |
|---|---|---|
| Lettuce leaves | 6 | 6 |
| Pink grapefruit, peeled, cut bite size | 1 | 1 |
| Papaya, peeled, cut bite size | 1 | 1 |
| Medium oranges, peeled, cut bite size | 2 | 2 |
| Can of pineapple chunks, drained and juice reserved | 14 oz. | 398 mL |
| Medium cooking apple, (such as McIntosh), cored and diced | 1 | 1 |
| Medium bananas, peeled and sliced | 2 | 2 |
| Reserved pineapple juice | | |
| Pomegranate seeds (or whole raspberries or blueberries), for garnish | | |

**Dressing:** Mix all 4 ingredients in small bowl. Cover. Chill until needed.

**Salad:** Line glass bowl with lettuce leaves.

Combine next 4 ingredients in large bowl.

Combine apple, banana and reserved pineapple juice in medium bowl. Toss to coat. Drain well. Add to rest of fruit. Toss. Turn into glass bowl.

Sprinkle with some pomegranate seeds. Serve with dressing on side. Serve remaining seeds in separate dish. Generously serves 8.

*1 serving: 229 Calories; 9.6 g Total Fat; 167 mg Sodium; 2 g Protein; 38 g Carbohydrate; 3 g Dietary Fiber*

Pictured on front cover.

# COCONUT MARSHMALLOW SALAD

*A showy rainbow of color.*

| | | |
|---|---|---|
| Miniature colored marshmallows | 1 cup | 250 mL |
| Can of fruit cocktail, drained | 14 oz. | 398 mL |
| Can of mandarin orange segments, drained | 10 oz. | 284 mL |
| Long thread unsweetened coconut (white or colored) | ¹/₂ cup | 125 mL |
| Maraschino cherries, halved (optional) | 6 | 6 |
| Non-fat sour cream (or non-fat plain yogurt) | 1 cup | 250 mL |

Combine marshmallows, drained fruits, coconut and cherry halves in large bowl. Stir.

Fold in sour cream. Cover. Chill for 30 minutes to allow flavors to meld and marshmallows to soften. Makes 4 cups (1 L), enough for 4 servings.

*1 serving: 184 Calories; 7.8 g Total Fat; 46 mg Sodium; 1 g Protein; 29 g Carbohydrate; 2 g Dietary Fiber*

## WALDORF SALAD

*A crunchy good salad with raisins and nuts.*

| | | |
|---|---|---|
| Large apples, with or without peel, diced | 2 | 2 |
| Chopped celery | ½ cup | 125 mL |
| Raisins (or currants) | ¼ cup | 60 mL |
| Chopped walnuts | ⅓ cup | 75 mL |
| Light salad dressing (or mayonnaise) | ⅓ cup | 75 mL |
| Milk | 1 tbsp. | 15 mL |

Combine first 4 ingredients in medium bowl.

Measure salad dressing into cup. Stir in milk. Pour over fruit mixture. Stir immediately to prevent apple from browning. Serves 4.

*1 serving: 220 Calories; 12.3 g Total Fat; 177 mg Sodium; 2 g Protein; 23 g Carbohydrate; 2 g Dietary Fiber*

## QUICK FRUIT SALAD

*Colorful and delicious. Not too sweet.*

| | | |
|---|---|---|
| Can of fruit cocktail, drained | 14 oz. | 398 mL |
| Miniature marshmallows | 2½ cups | 625 mL |
| Chopped walnuts | ¼ cup | 60 mL |
| Non-fat sour cream | 1 cup | 250 mL |
| Lettuce leaves | 4 | 4 |
| Maraschino cherries | 4 | 4 |

Mix first 4 ingredients in medium bowl. Let stand for at least 1 hour.

Place 1 lettuce leaf on each of 4 individual salad plates. Divide fruit mixture over lettuce leaves. Top each with cherry. Serves 4.

*1 serving: 207 Calories; 5.2 g Total Fat; 60 mg Sodium; 4 g Protein; 39 g Carbohydrate; 2 g Dietary Fiber*

## SPINACH FRUIT SALAD

*Refreshing, perfect for a hot summer day.*

| | | |
|---|---|---|
| Spinach (or romaine lettuce) leaves | 8-10 | 8-10 |
| Pink grapefruit sections | 6-8 | 6-8 |
| Kiwifruit slices | 6 | 6 |
| Toasted sliced almonds (see Tip, page 21) | 2 tsp. | 10 mL |
| **SWEET AND SOUR DRESSING** | | |
| White vinegar | 1 tsp. | 5 mL |
| Golden corn syrup | 2 tbsp. | 30 mL |
| Prepared mustard | 1 tsp. | 5 mL |

Fold spinach leaves over using 4 or 5 per plate. Make a row just off center of plate, overlapping ends so as to make an unbroken sort of ridge. Place grapefruit sections in a row in front of leaves. Place kiwifruit slices in a row in front of grapefruit. Sprinkle almonds over fruit.

**Sweet And Sour Dressing:** Stir vinegar, corn syrup and mustard together in small bowl. Drizzle over spinach and fruit. Serves 2.

*1 serving: 112 Calories; 1.5 g Total Fat; 58 mg Sodium; 2 g Protein; 25 g Carbohydrate; 3 g Dietary Fiber*

1. Peach Melba Salad, page 31
2. Jicama Fruit Salad, page 20

Props Courtesy Of:   Le Gnome, The Bay

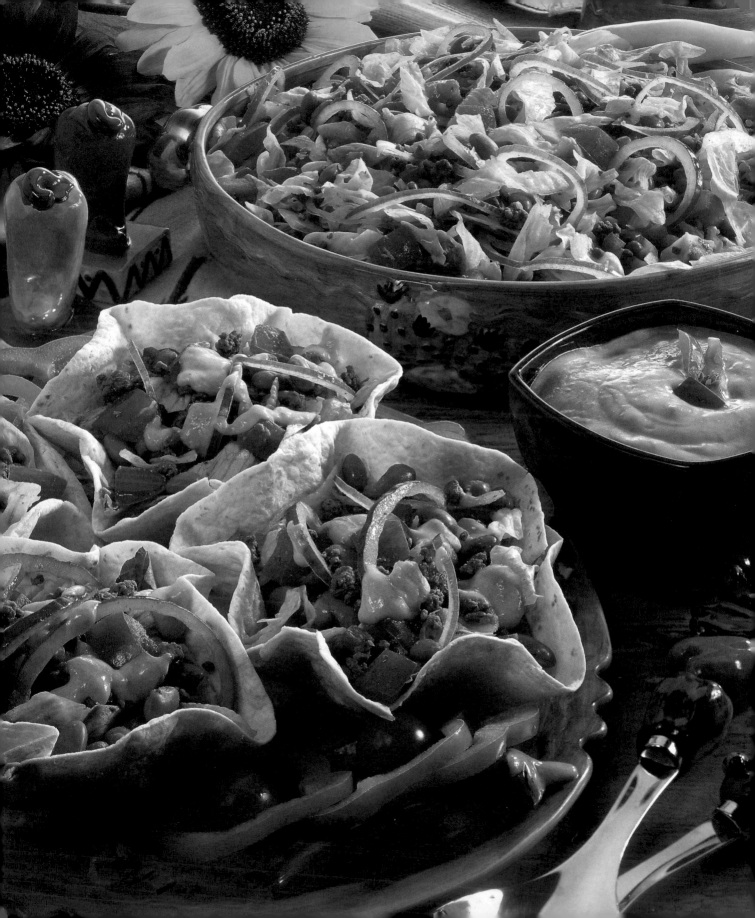

## MELON SALAD

*Makes a colorful salad. Leftovers can be made into a fruit shake.*

| | | |
|---|---|---|
| Peeled and seeded cantaloupe cubes | 1 cup | 250 mL |
| Peeled and seeded honeydew cubes | 1 cup | 250 mL |
| Peeled and seeded watermelon cubes | 1 cup | 250 mL |
| Medium banana, cut up | 1 | 1 |
| Non-fat peach yogurt | ½ cup | 125 mL |
| Non-fat plain or vanilla yogurt | 1 cup | 250 mL |

Combine fruits in serving bowl.

Mix both yogurts in small bowl. Drizzle over fruit. Serves 4.

*1 serving: 123 Calories; 0.6 g Total Fat; 78 mg Sodium; 6 g Protein; 26 g Carbohydrate; 1 g Dietary Fiber*

## SWEET WHEAT SALAD

*Fruit, grain and dairy—all this in a mouth-watering salad. Also makes a good dessert.*

| | | |
|---|---|---|
| Wheat kernels Boiling water, to cover | 1 cup | 250 mL |
| Cream cheese, softened | 8 oz. | 250 g |
| Can of crushed pineapple, with juice | 14 oz. | 398 mL |
| Instant vanilla pudding powder (4 serving size) | 1 | 1 |
| Lemon juice | 2 tbsp. | 30 mL |
| Frozen whipped topping, thawed | 4 cups | 1 L |
| Maraschino cherries, for garnish (optional) | | |

Cook wheat in boiling water in small saucepan for 1 hour until tender. Drain. Cool.

Beat cream cheese and pineapple with juice in medium bowl until mixed.

Beat in pudding powder and lemon juice. Add wheat. Stir.

Fold in whipped topping. Turn into serving bowl.

Garnish with cherries. Makes 8 cups (2 L), enough for 16 servings.

*1 serving: 196 Calories; 10.7 g Total Fat; 71 g Protein; 24 g Carbohydrate; 2 g Dietary Fiber*

Props Courtesy Of: Le Gnome, Stokes

1. Mexican Salad, page 26
2. Tortilla Bowls, page 26

## JICAMA FRUIT SALAD

*This makes a large salad. Halve the recipe for a smaller crowd.*

| LEMON POPPY SEED DRESSING | | |
|---|---|---|
| Non-fat lemon yogurt | 1 cup | 250 mL |
| Granulated sugar | 1 tsp. | 5 mL |
| Poppy seeds | 1 tsp. | 5 mL |
| Medium heads of butter lettuce, torn | 2 | 2 |
| Medium jicama, cut julienne | ½ | ½ |
| Sliced fresh strawberries | 2 cups | 500 mL |
| Can of mandarin orange segments, drained | 10 oz. | 284 mL |
| Can of pineapple tidbits, drained | 8 oz. | 227 mL |
| Miniature marshmallows | 1 cup | 250 mL |

**Lemon Poppy Seed Dressing:** Combine first 3 ingredients in small bowl. Stir until smooth.

Toss remaining 6 ingredients together in large bowl. Spoon onto individual plates. Drizzle dressing over each serving. Makes 16 cups (4 L), enough for 16 servings.

**1 serving:** *46 Calories; 0.3 g Total Fat; 17 mg Sodium; 2 g Protein; 10 g Carbohydrate; 2 g Dietary Fiber*

Pictured on page 17.

## ORANGE LETTUCE SALAD

*Most attractive. A hint of both sweet and sour in the dressing.*

| Torn assorted salad greens, lightly packed | 6 cups | 1.5 L |
|---|---|---|
| Can of mandarin orange segments, drained | 10 oz. | 284 mL |
| Toasted sliced almonds (see Tip, page 21) | ¼ cup | 60 mL |
| Bacon slices, cooked crisp and crumbled (optional) | 6 | 6 |
| DRESSING | | |
| White vinegar | 3 tbsp. | 50 mL |
| Granulated sugar | ¼ cup | 60 mL |
| Prepared mustard | ½ tsp. | 2 mL |
| Paprika | ½ tsp. | 2 mL |
| Cooking oil | 1 tbsp. | 15 mL |

Place first 4 ingredients in large bowl.

**Dressing:** Stir vinegar, sugar, mustard and paprika together in small bowl until sugar is dissolved.

Drizzle cooking oil over salad greens. Toss well. Add dressing. Toss to coat. Makes 8 cups (2 L), enough for 8 servings.

**1 serving:** *73 Calories; 3.5 g Total Fat; 10 mg Sodium; 1 g Protein; 11 g Carbohydrate; 1 g Dietary Fiber*

*Instead of croutons, coarsely crush corn chips and add to a salad just before tossing with the dressing.*

# SHRIMP SALAD

*Fruit wedges are topped with a yummy shrimp sauce.*

| | | |
|---|---|---|
| Small head of iceberg lettuce, shredded | 1 | 1 |
| Thin slices of cantaloupe (or papaya) | 32 | 32 |
| Thin slices of honeydew | 24 | 24 |
| TOPPING | | |
| Light salad dressing (or mayonnaise) | 3/4 cup | 175 mL |
| Chili sauce | 1/3 cup | 75 mL |
| Sweet pickle relish | 2 tbsp. | 30 mL |
| Onion powder | 1/4 tsp. | 1 mL |
| Cans of cocktail shrimp (4 oz., 113 g, each), drained and rinsed | 2 | 2 |

Divide and spread lettuce on 8 individual salad plates. Overlap 4 slices cantaloupe and 3 slices honeydew on each plate, beginning and ending with cantaloupe.

**Topping:** Combine first 4 ingredients in medium bowl. Stir.

Carefully fold in shrimp. Spoon over melons. Serves 8.

*1 serving: 172 Calories; 6.9 g Total Fat; 418 mg Sodium; 8 g Protein; 21 g Carbohydrate; 2 g Dietary Fiber*

# DRIED FRUIT COMPOTE

*Great for a barbecue or buffet table. Unusual and delicious.*

| | | |
|---|---|---|
| Dried mixed fruit (apricots, peaches and pears) | 12 oz. | 340 g |
| Water | 2 cups | 500 mL |
| Granulated sugar | 1/2 cup | 125 mL |
| Raisins | 1/4 cup | 60 mL |
| Lemon juice | 1 tsp. | 5 mL |
| Curry powder | 1 tsp. | 5 mL |
| Cornstarch | 1 tbsp. | 15 mL |
| Cold water | 1 tbsp. | 15 mL |

Cut dried apricots in half and peaches and pears into quarters. Combine fruits, water, sugar and raisins in medium saucepan. Bring to a boil. Cover. Simmer for 15 minutes. Remove to medium bowl.

Measure 1 cup (250 mL) juice from cooked fruit into same saucepan, adding more water if needed. Stir in lemon juice and curry powder. Heat to boiling.

Stir cornstarch into cold water in cup. Stir into hot juice mixture until boiling and thickened. Add cooked fruit. Stir to heat through. Serve hot. Serves 8.

*1 serving: 173 Calories; 0.3 g Total Fat; 9 mg Sodium; 1 g Protein; 45 g Carbohydrate; 3 g Dietary Fiber*

**Variation:** Omit curry powder. Add 1/2 tsp. (2 mL) cinnamon.

*To toast almonds, sesame seeds and pecans, place in single layer in ungreased shallow baking dish. Bake in 350°F (175°C) oven for 5 to 8 minutes, watching carefully so they don't burn.*

# Full Meal Salads

*a* salad for dinner? Well, why not? Here are some simple, hearty salads that offer the perfect alternative to cooking on a hot summer day, or whenever dinner must be a quick affair. Summertime Salad, page 25, has all the ingredients to make up a well-balanced, nutritious meal, and Pacific Rim Salad, page 24, presents an impressive flavor for everyone in your family to enjoy. Add a roll or bun, and your meal is complete.

## THAI CHICKEN SALAD

*Dressing may be drizzled over or tossed with this salad. Sprinkle with peanuts. A popular salad.*

| | | |
|---|---|---|
| Cooking oil | 2 tsp. | 10 mL |
| Boneless, skinless chicken breast halves (about 1 lb., 454 g) | 4 | 4 |
| Head of romaine lettuce, torn | 1 | 1 |
| Green onions, sliced | 3-4 | 3-4 |
| Chopped peanuts | ½ cup | 125 mL |
| **PEANUT SAUCE** | | |
| Smooth peanut butter | 3 tbsp. | 50 mL |
| Soy sauce | 1 tbsp. | 15 mL |
| Apple cider vinegar | 1 tbsp. | 15 mL |
| Water | ¼ cup | 60 mL |
| Granulated sugar | 1 tsp. | 5 mL |
| Cayenne pepper (or to taste) | ⅛ tsp. | 0.5 mL |

Heat cooking oil in frying pan. Add chicken. Brown both sides until no pink remains. Cut into short strips.

Divide lettuce among 6 individual plates. Sprinkle with chicken, green onion and peanuts.

**Peanut Sauce:** Mix all 6 ingredients in small bowl or shake in covered jar. Drizzle over salad. Makes a scant ⅔ cup (150 mL) sauce. Serves 6.

*1 serving:* 246 Calories; 14.2 g Total Fat; 261 mg Sodium; 24 g Protein; 7 g Carbohydrate; 2 g Dietary Fiber

Pictured on page 107.

# GINGER CHICKEN SALAD

*The orange and ginger flavors complement each other. Serve on a bed of lettuce or carrot strings.*

| | | |
|---|---|---|
| Boneless, skinless chicken breast halves (about 2), sliced paper-thin | ½ lb. | 225 g |
| Juice and finely grated peel of 1 medium orange | | |
| Low-sodium soy sauce | 1 tbsp. | 15 mL |
| Grated gingerroot | 2 tsp. | 10 mL |
| Frozen concentrated orange juice | 2 tbsp. | 30 mL |
| Ground ginger | 1 tsp. | 5 mL |
| Garlic powder | ⅛ tsp. | 0.5 mL |
| Ginger ale | ½ cup | 125 mL |
| Cornstarch | 1 tsp. | 5 mL |
| Cooked bow (farfalle) pasta (about 1 cup, 250 mL, uncooked) | 2 cups | 500 mL |
| Medium carrot, thinly peeled lengthwise into long ribbons | 1 | 1 |
| Green onion, sliced | 1 | 1 |
| Thinly sliced celery, cut on diagonal | ½ cup | 125 mL |
| Finely shredded red cabbage, lightly packed | 1 cup | 250 mL |
| Medium orange or yellow peppers, slivered | 2 | 2 |

Place first 4 ingredients in small bowl. Stir. Let stand for 15 minutes. Heat non-stick frying pan or wok on medium-high. Add chicken mixture. Stir-fry for 10 minutes until chicken is no longer pink and most of liquid is evaporated.

Combine next 5 ingredients in cup. Stir. Add to chicken mixture. Stir until mixture comes to a boil. Boil for 1 minute until slightly thickened. Remove from heat. Cool.

Combine remaining 6 ingredients in large bowl. Add chicken mixture. Stir well. Serve immediately or chill. Makes 6 cups (1.5 L), enough for 6 servings.

*1 serving: 158 Calories; 1 g Total Fat; 148 mg Sodium; 12 g Protein; 27 g Carbohydrate; 4 g Dietary Fiber*

Pictured on page 72.

*Cook chicken thoroughly because heat destroys bacteria. Test for doneness by piercing the chicken with a fork. If the juices run clear, with no tinge of pink, it's done.*

## PACIFIC RIM SALAD

*Great mixture. Great flavor. Great color.*

| | | |
|---|---|---|
| Chopped iceberg lettuce, lightly packed | 4 cups | 1 L |
| Fresh bean sprouts | 1 cup | 250 mL |
| Cooked chicken, cut bite size | 1 cup | 250 mL |
| Slivered green pepper | ¼ cup | 60 mL |
| Slivered red pepper | ¼ cup | 60 mL |
| Slivered yellow pepper | ¼ cup | 60 mL |
| Sliced water chestnuts | ¼ cup | 60 mL |
| Julienned carrot | ¼ cup | 60 mL |
| Chopped green onion | 2 tbsp. | 30 mL |
| Cooking oil | 2 tbsp. | 30 mL |
| Wonton wrappers | 8 | 8 |
| **HOISIN DRESSING** | | |
| Hoisin sauce | ¼ cup | 60 mL |
| Cooking oil | 1 tbsp. | 15 mL |
| White vinegar | 1 tbsp. | 15 mL |
| Toasted sliced almonds (see Tip, page 21) | ¼ cup | 60 mL |

Combine first 9 ingredients in large bowl.

Heat cooking oil in frying pan until hot. Cut wonton wrappers into ½ inch (12 mm) strips. Cut each strip into 2 pieces. Fry until crisp and browned. Drain on paper towels.

**Hoisin Dressing:** Mix first 3 ingredients in small bowl. Pour dressing over salad in large bowl when ready to serve.

Add wonton wrappers and almonds. Toss. Serves 8.

*1 serving: 138 Calories; 7.7 g Total Fat; 392 mg Sodium; 8 g Protein; 10 g Carbohydrate; 1 g Dietary Fiber*

Pictured on page 53.

## TURKEY SALAD

*Great for Boxing Day.*

| | | |
|---|---|---|
| Diced cooked turkey | 4 cups | 1 L |
| Seedless grapes, halved | 1 cup | 250 mL |
| Sliced celery | 1 cup | 250 mL |
| Can of mandarin orange segments, drained | 10 oz. | 284 mL |
| Toasted slivered almonds (see Tip, page 21) | ½ cup | 125 mL |
| Diced apple, with peel | 1 cup | 250 mL |
| Chopped peeled cucumber | 1 cup | 250 mL |
| Fresh bean sprouts | 2 cups | 500 mL |
| **ORANGE DRESSING** | | |
| Light salad dressing (or mayonnaise) | ½ cup | 125 mL |
| White vinegar | 2 tbsp. | 30 mL |
| Frozen concentrated orange juice | 1 tbsp. | 15 mL |
| Granulated sugar | 1 tbsp. | 15 mL |
| Salt | ½ tsp. | 2 mL |
| Onion powder | ¼ tsp. | 1 mL |

Put first 8 ingredients into large bowl.

**Orange Dressing:** Stir all 6 ingredients together in small bowl. Makes ¾ cup (175 mL) dressing. Add to salad. Toss well. Serves 6 to 8.

*1 serving: 305 Calories; 12.4 g Total Fat; 458 mg Sodium; 28 g Protein; 22 g Carbohydrate; 3 g Dietary Fiber*

# SUMMERTIME SALAD

*A great luncheon meal. Make the dressing the day before. Cover and chill until ready to use. Shake well.*

| Julienned cooked lean beef | 3 cups | 750 mL |
| Sliced fresh green beans, steamed | 1 cup | 250 mL |
| Sliced cucumber, with peel | ½ cup | 125 mL |
| Diced celery | 1½ cups | 375 mL |
| Diced green pepper | ½ cup | 125 mL |
| Baby new potatoes, boiled and diced | 1 lb. | 454 g |
| Finely chopped green onion | ¼ cup | 60 mL |
| Chopped fresh parsley | 3 tbsp. | 50 mL |
| **BALSAMIC DRESSING** | | |
| Olive oil | ⅓ cup | 75 mL |
| Balsamic vinegar | 2 tbsp. | 30 mL |
| Salt | ¾ tsp. | 4 mL |
| Small garlic clove, minced | 1 | 1 |
| Dijon mustard | 1½ tsp. | 7 mL |
| Dried tarragon | ¼ tsp. | 1 mL |
| Torn assorted salad greens, lightly packed | 6 cups | 1.5 L |

Combine first 8 ingredients in large bowl.

**Balsamic Dressing:** Combine first 6 ingredients in large bowl. Toss with vegetable mixture. Chill for at least 1 hour to blend flavors.

Serve on bed of salad greens. Serves 6.

*1 serving: 291 Calories; 16.4 g Total Fat; 407 mg Sodium; 23 g Protein; 14 g Carbohydrate; 2 g Dietary Fiber*

# BEEF AND SPINACH SALAD

*Prepare the vegetables while the steak is cooking.*

| Cooking oil | 1 tbsp. | 15 mL |
| Garlic cloves, minced | 2 | 2 |
| Salt | ½ tsp. | 2 mL |
| Freshly ground pepper | ½ tsp. | 2 mL |
| Top sirloin steak (¾ inch, 2 cm, thick) | 1 lb. | 454 g |
| Torn spinach, lightly packed | 10 cups | 2.5 L |
| Grated carrot | 1 cup | 250 mL |
| Sliced fresh mushrooms | 1½ cups | 375 mL |
| Light creamy dressing (your favorite) | ⅓ cup | 75 mL |
| Croutons, for garnish | | |
| Bacon slices, cooked crisp and crumbled, for garnish | | |

Combine cooking oil, garlic, salt and pepper in small bowl. Spread over both sides of steak. Heat medium non-stick frying pan until hot. Cook each side of steak for 5 to 7 minutes until desired doneness. Trim off fat. Cut steak lengthwise in half and then crosswise into ¼ inch (6 mm) slices.

Toss spinach, carrot, mushrooms and dressing in large serving bowl. Arrange sliced beef on top.

Sprinkle with croutons and bacon bits. Serve immediately. Serves 4.

*1 serving: 257 Calories; 11.2 g Total Fat; 711 mg Sodium; 28 g Protein; 13 g Carbohydrate; 5 g Dietary Fiber*

## Tortilla Bowls

*Make as many tortilla bowls as you need. The microwave method is better for corn tortillas—they tend to crack in the oven.*

| | | |
|---|---|---|
| **Corn (or flour) tortilla, 6 or 7 inch (15 or 18 cm) size** | 1 | 1 |

**Microwave Oven Method:** Lightly grease bottom and outside of 2 cup (500 mL) microwave-safe liquid measure. Turn measure upside down. Press tortilla over bottom and sides. Microwave on high (100%) for 1 minute. Using oven mitts, again press tortilla around measure. Microwave on high (100%) for about 1 minute until brown spots begin to appear. Press tortilla against measure again, if necessary. Turn out onto rack to cool. Makes 1.

**Conventional Oven Method:** Lightly grease bottom and outside of 2 cup (500 mL) ovenproof liquid measure. Turn measure upside down onto baking sheet. Press tortilla over bottom and sides. Bake in 325°F (160°C) oven for 7 to 10 minutes until brown spots appear, occasionally pressing tortilla against measure. Makes 1.

*1 tortilla bowl: 89 Calories; 1.5 g Total Fat; 71 mg Sodium; 3 g Protein; 17 g Carbohydrate; 1 g Dietary Fiber*

Pictured on page 18.

**Note:** For larger bowl, use 10 inch (25 cm) flour tortilla over 4 cup (1 L) liquid measure.

## Mexican Salad

*Pinto is Spanish for "painted." The pinto bean has streaks of reddish brown on a pale pink background. If tortilla bowls are not being used, toss the dressing in the bowl with the lettuce mixture.*

| | | |
|---|---|---|
| Lean ground beef | ½ lb. | 225 g |
| Taco seasoning mix | 4 tsp. | 20 mL |
| Water | ½ cup | 125 mL |
| Can of pinto beans, drained | 14 oz. | 398 mL |
| Shredded iceberg lettuce, lightly packed | 4 cups | 1 L |
| Small red pepper, diced | 1 | 1 |
| Very thinly sliced red onion | 1 cup | 250 mL |
| Medium tomato, diced | 1 | 1 |
| Tortilla Bowls, this page | 6 | 6 |
| **CHILI DRESSING** | | |
| Non-fat plain yogurt | ½ cup | 125 mL |
| Non-fat sour cream | ½ cup | 125 mL |
| Chili sauce | 3 tbsp. | 50 mL |
| Onion powder | ½ tsp. | 2 mL |
| Garlic powder | ⅛ tsp. | 0.5 mL |
| Salt | ¼ tsp. | 1 mL |

Scramble-fry ground beef in non-stick frying pan until no pink remains. Drain. Stir in taco seasoning and water. Simmer until all liquid is evaporated. Cool to room temperature.

Combine pinto beans, lettuce, red pepper, red onion and tomato in medium bowl. Toss together. Stir in beef mixture.

Fill tortilla bowls.

**Chili Dressing:** Combine all 6 ingredients in small bowl. Drizzle dressing over salad. Stir to mix. Makes 6 cups (1.5 L), enough for 6 servings.

*1 serving: 149 Calories; 3.7 g Total Fat; 721 mg Sodium; 12 g Protein; 18 g Carbohydrate; 3 g Dietary Fiber*

Pictured on page 18.

## MANGO TANGO SALAD

*Marinate the steak overnight. Prepare the rest of the salad in the morning.*

| Sirloin (or round) steak | 1 lb. | 454 g |
|---|---|---|
| Dry (or alcohol-free) red wine | ½ cup | 125 mL |
| Penne (or fusilli) pasta | 2 cups | 500 mL |
| Boiling water | 3 qts. | 3 L |
| Cooking oil (optional) | 1 tbsp. | 15 mL |
| Salt | 2 tsp. | 10 mL |
| Hot mango chutney | 1 cup | 250 mL |
| Cooking oil | 2 tsp. | 10 mL |
| Sesame oil | 1 tsp. | 5 mL |
| Lemon juice | ¼ cup | 60 mL |
| Frozen peas | 1½ cups | 375 mL |
| Large carrot, cut julienne | 1 | 1 |
| Diced ripe mango | ½ cup | 125 mL |
| Toasted sesame seeds (see Tip, page 21) | 2 tbsp. | 30 mL |

Lightly score both surfaces of steak. Place in shallow dish or sealable plastic bag. Pour in wine. Turn to coat well. Cover or seal. Marinate in refrigerator for at least 2 hours, turning several times. Remove steak. Discard wine. Broil each side of steak for 5 to 6 minutes until desired doneness. Thinly slice across grain.

Cook pasta in boiling water, first amount of cooking oil and salt in large uncovered pot or Dutch oven for 5 to 7 minutes until tender but firm. Drain. Rinse with cold water. Drain. Return to pot.

Mix chutney, both oils and lemon juice in small bowl. Add to pasta. Add steak, frozen peas, carrot and mango. Chill for 3 to 4 hours.

Toss with sesame seeds just before serving. Serves 4.

*1 serving:* 507 Calories; 10.9 g Total Fat; 118 mg Sodium; 33 g Protein; 68 g Carbohydrate; 6 g Dietary Fiber

Pictured on page 71.

## APPLE AND BEEF SALAD

*Use unpeeled boiled new potatoes, halved or quartered for real visual appeal. Makes a satisfying luncheon salad.*

| Cooked lean beef, cut into ½ inch (12 mm) cubes | 3 cups | 750 mL |
|---|---|---|
| Coarsely diced cooked potato | 3 cups | 750 mL |
| Finely chopped celery | ½ cup | 125 mL |
| Medium green pepper, finely chopped | 1 | 1 |
| Grated Colby cheese | 1 cup | 250 mL |
| Medium apples, with peel, diced into ½ inch (12 mm) pieces | 2 | 2 |
| Lemon juice | 1 tsp. | 5 mL |
| **DILL DRESSING** | | |
| Light salad dressing (or mayonnaise) | ½ cup | 125 mL |
| Milk | ¼ cup | 60 mL |
| Dill weed | 1 tsp. | 5 mL |
| Salt | ½ tsp. | 2 mL |
| Pepper, to taste | | |

Combine first 5 ingredients in large bowl.

Toss apple and lemon juice in small bowl. Add to beef mixture. Mix.

**Dill Dressing:** Combine salad dressing, milk, dill weed, salt and pepper in small bowl. Makes ¾ cup (175 mL) dressing. Add to beef mixture. Toss gently. Serves 6.

*1 serving:* 374 Calories; 17.1 g Total Fat; 551 mg Sodium; 28 g Protein; 27 g Carbohydrate; 2 g Dietary Fiber

## FAR EAST BEEF SALAD

*Prepare the dressing and vegetables while the steak is broiling.*

| | | |
|---|---|---|
| Sirloin (or round) steak | 1 lb. | 454 g |
| Light French dressing | ¼ cup | 60 mL |
| | | |
| Light French dressing | ¾ cup | 175 mL |
| Soy sauce | ¼ cup | 60 mL |
| Brown sugar, packed | 1½ tbsp. | 25 mL |
| Dried crushed chilies | ¼ tsp. | 1 mL |
| | | |
| Thinly shredded savoy cabbage, lightly packed | 4 cups | 1 L |
| Small red onion, finely sliced | 1 | 1 |
| | | |
| Toasted sesame seeds (see Tip, page 21) | 2 tbsp. | 30 mL |
| Chopped fresh cilantro (coriander) | 2 tbsp. | 30 mL |
| | | |
| Cantaloupe slices, for garnish | | |

Coat steak with first amount of dressing. Place on broiler pan. Broil each side of steak for 3 to 4 minutes until desired doneness. Thinly slice across grain. Reserve any drippings.

Heat second amount of dressing, soy sauce, brown sugar, reserved drippings and crushed chilies in medium saucepan. Add steak slices. Mix.

Arrange cabbage and red onion in large bowl or on 4 individual salad plates. Cover with steak mixture.

Sprinkle with sesame seeds and cilantro.

Surround with cantaloupe slices. Serve immediately. Serves 4.

*1 serving: 322 Calories; 13.6 g Total Fat; 2451 mg Sodium; 27 g Protein; 25 g Carbohydrate; 4 g Dietary Fiber*

## BEEF SALAD

*Fresh tasting, dilly and creamy.*

| | | |
|---|---|---|
| Julienned cooked roast beef | 2 cups | 500 mL |
| Chopped peeled cucumber | 1 cup | 250 mL |
| Radishes, sliced or diced | 6 | 6 |
| Chopped celery | ½ cup | 125 mL |
| Cooked peas | 1 cup | 250 mL |
| Torn iceberg lettuce, lightly packed | 4 cups | 1 L |
| **CREAMY DILL DRESSING** | | |
| Non-fat sour cream | 1 cup | 250 mL |
| Dill weed | 1 tsp. | 5 mL |
| Salt | ½ tsp. | 2 mL |
| Milk | 1 tbsp. | 15 mL |
| Granulated sugar | ½ tsp. | 2 mL |

Combine first 6 ingredients in large bowl.

**Creamy Dill Dressing:** Combine all 5 ingredients in small bowl. Chill for at least 30 minutes. Pour over salad just before serving. Toss to coat. Serves 4.

*1 serving: 195 Calories; 4.3 g Total Fat; 476 mg Sodium; 26 g Protein; 13 g Carbohydrate; 3 g Dietary Fiber*

*To remove the core from a head of lettuce, hit the core end once sharply against the countertop. The core then twists out easily.*

## CRAB LOUIS

*Makes a great luncheon dish. Tart dressing really sets it off.*

**LOUIS DRESSING**

| | | |
|---|---|---|
| Chili sauce | 1/3 cup | 75 mL |
| Light salad dressing (or mayonnaise) | 1/3 cup | 75 mL |
| Granulated sugar | 1/4 tsp. | 1 mL |
| Salt | 1/4 tsp. | 1 mL |
| Prepared mustard | 1/4 tsp. | 1 mL |
| White vinegar | 1 tbsp. | 15 mL |
| Onion powder | 1/8 tsp. | 0.5 mL |
| Milk | 3 tbsp. | 50 mL |
| Small head of iceberg lettuce, shredded | 1 | 1 |
| Cans of crabmeat (4 1/4 oz., 120 g, each), drained, cartilage removed | 2 | 2 |
| Large hard-boiled eggs, quartered lengthwise | 6 | 6 |
| Tomato slices | 6 | 6 |

**Louis Dressing:** Mix first 8 ingredients well in small bowl. Makes 3/4 cup (175 mL) dressing.

Divide lettuce among 6 individual salad plates. Flake crabmeat. Divide over lettuce.

Arrange egg wedges around edge of plates. Place tomato slice in center. Drizzle with a bit of dressing. Serve remaining dressing in small bowl. Serves 6.

*1 serving: 177 Calories; 9.4 g Total Fat; 768 mg Sodium; 13 g Protein; 10 g Carbohydrate; 2 g Dietary Fiber*

## CRAB SALAD

*Delicious luncheon salad. Prepare ahead and assemble at the last minute.*

| | | |
|---|---|---|
| Cans of crabmeat (4 1/4 oz., 120 g, each), drained, cartilage removed | 2 | 2 |
| Large hard-boiled eggs, chopped | 3 | 3 |
| Thinly sliced celery | 1/2 cup | 125 mL |
| Chopped pimiento | 1 tbsp. | 15 mL |
| Salt, sprinkle | | |
| Pepper, sprinkle | | |
| Chopped iceberg lettuce, lightly packed | 6 cups | 1.5 L |

**CREAMY DRESSING**

| | | |
|---|---|---|
| Light salad dressing (or mayonnaise) | 3/4 cup | 175 mL |
| Milk | 3 tbsp. | 50 mL |
| Granulated sugar | 1/2 tsp. | 2 mL |
| Seasoned salt | 1/2 tsp. | 2 mL |
| Paprika | 1/2 tsp. | 2 mL |

Combine first 6 ingredients in medium bowl.

Put lettuce into large bowl.

**Creamy Dressing:** Stir salad dressing, milk, sugar, seasoned salt and paprika together in small bowl. Reserve 1/3 of dressing. Pour 2/3 of dressing over lettuce just before serving. Toss together. Divide among 4 individual plates. Divide crabmeat mixture over lettuce. Drizzle with remaining 1/3 of dressing. Serves 4.

*1 serving: 255 Calories; 16.7 g Total Fat; 993 mg Sodium; 14 g Protein; 12 g Carbohydrate; 1 g Dietary Fiber*

# Molded Salads

**M**olded salads were once created using calfs' hoof jelly, but today we see them more often prepared with unflavored and flavored gelatins. Their presence at the table is both colorful and eye-catching, and despite the arrival of more exotic salads and dressings, they continue to be a traditional favorite at family gatherings.

## TOMATO SHRIMP ASPIC

*Glossy red with celery and shrimp peeking through.*

| | | |
|---|---|---|
| Tomato juice | 2$\frac{1}{2}$ cups | 625 mL |
| Small bay leaf | 1 | 1 |
| Onion powder | $\frac{1}{2}$ tsp. | 2 mL |
| Envelopes unflavored gelatin ($\frac{1}{4}$ oz., 7 g, each) | 2 | 2 |
| Cold water | $\frac{1}{2}$ cup | 125 mL |
| Granulated sugar | 3 tbsp. | 50 mL |
| Salt | $\frac{3}{4}$ tsp. | 4 mL |
| Paprika | $\frac{1}{4}$ tsp. | 1 mL |
| Chopped celery | $\frac{3}{4}$ cup | 175 mL |
| Can of small shrimp, drained and rinsed | 4 oz. | 113 g |

Put tomato juice, bay leaf and onion powder into medium saucepan. Heat. Simmer for 5 minutes. Discard bay leaf.

Sprinkle gelatin over cold water in small saucepan. Let stand for 1 minute. Heat, stirring until gelatin is dissolved. Add to tomato juice.

Stir in sugar, salt and paprika until sugar is dissolved. Chill, stirring and scraping down sides often, until mixture shows signs of thickening.

Fold in celery and shrimp. Turn into 3 cup (750 mL) mold. Chill until firm. Serves 6 to 8.

***1 serving:*** *73 Calories; 0.4 g Total Fat; 759 mg Sodium; 7 g Protein; 12 g Carbohydrate; 1 g Dietary Fiber*

# Cucumber Mousse

*A bit of crunch from cucumber. A mild hint of pickle adds to flavor. A good make-the-day-before salad. Prepare cucumber first so it will have plenty of time to drain.*

| | | |
|---|---|---|
| Packages lemon-flavored gelatin (jelly powder), 3 oz. (85 g), each | 2 | 2 |
| Salt | 2 tsp. | 10 mL |
| Boiling water | 1²/₃ cups | 400 mL |
| White vinegar | 3 tbsp. | 50 mL |
| Onion powder | ¹/₂ tsp. | 2 mL |
| Sour cream | 1 cup | 250 mL |
| Salad dressing (or mayonnaise) | ¹/₂ cup | 125 mL |
| Finely chopped cucumber, with peel, well drained | 2 cups | 500 mL |

Combine gelatin, salt and boiling water in medium bowl. Stir until gelatin is dissolved.

Add vinegar and onion powder. Stir. Chill, stirring and scraping down sides of bowl often, until mixture shows signs of thickening.

Add sour cream and salad dressing. Stir to blend. Fold in cucumber. Turn into 4 cup (1 L) mold. Chill. Serves 8.

*1 serving: 207 Calories; 11.9 g Total Fat; 850 mg Sodium; 3 g Protein; 23 g Carbohydrate; trace Dietary Fiber*

*Spraying salad molds with no-stick cooking spray before adding the salad makes them easier to remove.*

# Peach Melba Salad

*Pretty enough—and sweet enough—for salad or dessert! Serve on shredded lettuce for salad. Make first thing in the morning. Keep chilled until serving time.*

| | | |
|---|---|---|
| Packages raspberry-flavored gelatin (jelly powder), 3 oz. (85 g), each | 2 | 2 |
| Boiling water | 1 cup | 250 mL |
| Can of peach pie filling | 19 oz. | 540 mL |
| Frozen whole raspberries, thawed | 10 oz. | 300 g |
| Lemon juice | 1 tsp. | 5 mL |
| **TOPPING** | | |
| Non-fat peach yogurt | 1 cup | 250 mL |
| Envelope dessert topping (not prepared) | 1 | 1 |
| Milk | ¹/₃ cup | 75 mL |

Stir gelatin into boiling water in medium bowl until dissolved.

Stir in pie filling, raspberries and lemon juice. Pour into 9 x 9 inch (22 x 22 cm) pan lightly sprayed. Chill until firm.

**Topping:** Stir yogurt vigorously in small bowl until smooth. Beat dessert topping and milk on low in separate small bowl. Beat on medium until stiff. Add to yogurt. Stir together well. Spread or pipe over jellied salad. Chill for 30 minutes. Cuts into 12 medium-size pieces.

*1 piece: 151 Calories; 1.7 g Total Fat; 63 mg Sodium; 3 g Protein; 33 g Carbohydrate; 2 g Dietary Fiber*

Pictured on page 17.

## Green Pepper Salad

*This two-tone salad is so festive! Its refreshing flavor works well with turkey or beef. A great addition to a buffet.*

| | | |
|---|---|---|
| Package lime-flavored gelatin (jelly powder) | 3 oz. | 85 g |
| Boiling water | 1 cup | 250 mL |
| Package lime-flavored gelatin (jelly powder) | 3 oz. | 85 g |
| Boiling water | 1 cup | 250 mL |
| Cold water | ¾ cup | 175 mL |
| Light salad dressing (or mayonnaise) | ½ cup | 125 mL |
| White vinegar | 1 tsp. | 5 mL |
| Finely chopped green pepper | 1 cup | 250 mL |
| Finely chopped celery | ½ cup | 125 mL |
| 1% creamed cottage cheese | 1 cup | 250 mL |

Stir first amount of gelatin into first amount of boiling water in medium bowl until dissolved. Chill, stirring and scraping down sides often, until gelatin shows signs of thickening.

As soon as first gelatin goes into refrigerator, stir second amount of gelatin into second amount of boiling water in another medium bowl until dissolved. Add cold water. Stir. Chill, stirring and scraping down sides often, until gelatin shows signs of thickening.

To first gelatin, stir in salad dressing and vinegar. Add green pepper, celery and cottage cheese. Stir. Turn into 6 cup (1.5 L) mold. Chill. When first gelatin is beginning to thicken, pour second gelatin over top in mold. Chill. Serves 8 to 10.

*1 serving:* 151 Calories; 4.3 g Total Fat; 313 mg Sodium; 6 g Protein; 23 g Carbohydrate; trace Dietary Fiber

## Cheesy Salad Mold

*Unusual and good. Olives don't overpower other ingredients. A different combination of fruit and nuts. Crunchy.*

| | | |
|---|---|---|
| Package lemon-flavored gelatin (jelly powder) | 3 oz. | 85 g |
| Boiling water | 1 cup | 250 mL |
| Reserved pineapple juice, plus cold water to make | 1 cup | 250 mL |
| Light frozen whipped topping, thawed | 1 cup | 250 mL |
| Finely chopped nuts | ½ cup | 125 mL |
| Grated light Cheddar cheese | 1 cup | 250 mL |
| Can of crushed pineapple, drained and juice reserved | 14 oz. | 398 mL |
| Sliced pimiento-stuffed olives | ½ cup | 125 mL |

Dissolve gelatin in boiling water in large bowl. Add reserved pineapple juice and cold water. Chill until slightly thickened. Beat until fluffy.

Fold in whipped topping. Fold in nuts, cheese, pineapple and olives. Pour into pretty serving bowl or 4 cup (1 L) mold. Serves 8 to 10.

*1 serving:* 204 Calories; 10.7 g Total Fat; 363 mg Sodium; 6 g Protein; 22 g Carbohydrate; 1 g Dietary Fiber

Pictured on page 35 and back cover.

# Pasta Salads

**P**asta is a low-fat ingredient, and so what better place to find it than in a nutritious salad. When you need to plan ahead, Macaroni Salad, page 39, can be prepared in advance and stored in the refrigerator overnight. For a quick and easy lunch, try Oriental Pasta Salad, page 38.

## VEGETABLE PASTA SALAD

*Brightly colored with red and green strips of pepper and zucchini.*

| Rotini pasta (8 oz., 225 g) | 3 cups | 750 mL |
|---|---|---|
| Boiling water | 3 qts. | 3 L |
| Cooking oil (optional) | 1 tbsp. | 15 mL |
| Salt | 2 tsp. | 10 mL |
| Medium red pepper, slivered | 1 | 1 |
| Slivered zucchini, with peel | 2 cups | 500 mL |
| Sliced green onion | ¼ cup | 60 mL |
| Fresh mushrooms, sliced | 6 | 6 |
| Sliced celery | ½ cup | 125 mL |
| Cooking oil | ⅓ cup | 75 mL |
| Red wine vinegar | ¼ cup | 60 mL |
| Grated Parmesan cheese | 2 tbsp. | 30 mL |
| Salt | 1 tsp. | 5 mL |
| Pepper | ¼ tsp. | 1 mL |
| Ground oregano | ¼ tsp. | 1 mL |
| Dried sweet basil | ¼ tsp. | 1 mL |
| Garlic powder | ¼ tsp. | 1 mL |

Cook pasta in boiling water, first amounts of cooking oil and salt in large uncovered pot or Dutch oven for 5 to 7 minutes, stirring occasionally, until tender but firm. Drain. Rinse with cold water. Drain well. Turn pasta into large bowl.

Add next 5 ingredients. Mix.

Mix remaining 8 ingredients in small bowl. Add to pasta mixture. Toss well. Makes 8 cups (2 L), enough for 8 servings.

*1 serving: 223 Calories; 10.7 g Total Fat; 380 mg Sodium; 6 g Protein; 27 g Carbohydrate; 2 g Dietary Fiber*

## BASIL CREAM FIESTA

*A cool refreshing salad on a warm summer day.*

| | | |
|---|---|---|
| Tri-colored fusilli (spiral) pasta (8 oz., 225 g) | 2²/₃ cups | 650 mL |
| Boiling water | 3 qts. | 3 L |
| Cooking oil | 2 tsp. | 10 mL |
| Salt | 1 tbsp. | 15 mL |
| Broccoli florets | 2 cups | 500 mL |
| Cauliflower florets | 2 cups | 500 mL |
| Thinly sliced carrot | 1 cup | 250 mL |
| Diced green pepper | ½ cup | 125 mL |
| Diced red or yellow pepper | ½ cup | 125 mL |
| Green onions, sliced | 2 | 2 |
| Non-fat plain yogurt | ½ cup | 125 mL |
| Non-fat sour cream | ½ cup | 125 mL |
| White (or alcohol-free) wine | ¼ cup | 60 mL |
| Basil pesto | 1 tbsp. | 15 mL |
| Garlic clove, minced | 1 | 1 |
| Dry mustard | ½ tsp. | 2 mL |
| Dried whole oregano, crushed | ½ tsp. | 2 mL |
| Salt | 1 tsp. | 5 mL |
| Freshly ground pepper, sprinkle | | |
| Halved cherry tomatoes (or diced tomato) | 1 cup | 250 mL |

Cook pasta in boiling water, cooking oil and first amount of salt in large uncovered pot or Dutch oven for 7 to 9 minutes, stirring occasionally, until pasta is tender but firm. Do not drain.

Add broccoli, cauliflower and carrot. Bring to a boil. Boil for 1 minute. Drain. Rinse with cold water. Drain well. Place in large bowl.

Add peppers and green onion. Toss.

Combine next 9 ingredients in small bowl. Mix until smooth. Add to pasta mixture. Stir gently to coat. Cover. Chill until ready to serve.

Place tomato halves over individual servings. Makes 10 cups (2.5 L), enough for 10 servings.

*1 serving: 129 Calories; 1.4 g Total Fat; 308 mg Sodium; 5 g Protein; 23 g Carbohydrate; 2 g Dietary Fiber*

Pictured on page 36.

1. Mixed Salad, page 57
2. Rice Salad, page 47
3. Cheesy Salad Mold, page 32

Props Courtesy Of: The Bay, X/S Wares

## LITTLE STUFFED TOMATOES

*Firm and fleshy roma tomatoes make great "shells" to contain filling.*

| | | |
|---|---|---|
| Firm small roma (plum) tomatoes | 8 | 8 |
| Salt | ½ tsp. | 2 mL |
| Tiny bow pasta | ⅔ cup | 150 mL |
| Boiling water | 4 cups | 1 L |
| Cooking oil (optional) | 1 tsp. | 5 mL |
| Salt | 1 tsp. | 5 mL |
| Non-fat spreadable herb and garlic-flavored cream cheese | ¼ cup | 60 mL |
| Non-fat sour cream | ¼ cup | 60 mL |
| Finely chopped cucumber, with peel | ½ cup | 125 mL |
| Finely chopped green onion | 1 tbsp. | 15 mL |
| Finely chopped fresh sweet basil | 2 tsp. | 10 mL |
| Chopped fresh parsley | 2 tsp. | 10 mL |
| Salt | ½ tsp. | 2 mL |
| Freshly ground pepper, sprinkle | | |

Cut tomatoes in half lengthwise. Scoop out inner pulp, discarding juice and seeds. Measure ½ cup (125 mL) pulp, discarding any extra. Sprinkle insides of tomatoes with first amount of salt. Turn upside down on paper towel. Let stand for 30 minutes to drain. Blot insides of tomato halves with paper towel to dry well.

Cook pasta in boiling water, cooking oil and second amount of salt in medium uncovered saucepan for 6 to 7 minutes, stirring occasionally, until tender but firm. Drain. Rinse with cold water. Drain well.

Combine cream cheese and sour cream in medium bowl. Mix until smooth. Stir in pasta. Add reserved tomato flesh, cucumber, green onion, basil, parsley, third amount of salt and pepper. Mix well. Cover. Chill until tomatoes are ready to be filled. Spoon a rounded tablespoonful of filling into each tomato half. Makes 16.

*1 filled tomato half: 32 Calories; 0.3 g Total Fat; 177 mg Sodium; 1 g Protein; 7 g Carbohydrate; 1 g Dietary Fiber*

*Before peeling and coring fruits and vegetables, line a dry sink with a few layers of newspaper. Discard the scraps on this paper as you work. When finished, cleanup is simple—just wrap up the paper and throw it in the trash!*

Props Courtesy Of: Le Gnome,
The Bay,
X/S Wares

# ORIENTAL PASTA SALAD

*Assemble in only 15 minutes!*

| | | |
|---|---|---|
| Vermicelli pasta | 6 oz. | 170 g |
| Boiling water | 6 cups | 1.5 L |
| Cooking oil (optional) | 2 tsp. | 10 mL |
| Salt | 1½ tsp. | 7 mL |
| Very thinly sliced green or red cabbage, lightly packed | 3 cups | 750 mL |
| Can of sliced water chestnuts, drained | 8 oz. | 227 mL |
| Celery rib, thinly sliced on diagonal | 1 | 1 |
| Medium red or yellow pepper, slivered | 1 | 1 |
| Thinly sliced fresh mushrooms | 1 cup | 250 mL |
| Green onions, thinly sliced | 2 | 2 |
| **ORIENTAL DRESSING** | | |
| Rice vinegar | 3 tbsp. | 50 mL |
| Sherry (or alcohol-free sherry) | 1 tbsp. | 15 mL |
| Low-sodium soy sauce | 1 tbsp. | 15 mL |
| Hoisin sauce | 1 tbsp. | 15 mL |
| Granulated sugar | 1 tsp. | 5 mL |
| Sesame oil | 2 tsp. | 10 mL |
| Toasted sesame seeds (see Tip, page 21) | 2 tsp. | 10 mL |

Cook pasta in boiling water, cooking oil and salt in large uncovered pot or Dutch oven for 5 to 6 minutes, stirring occasionally, until tender but firm. Drain. Rinse with cold water. Drain well. Turn pasta into large bowl.

Add next 6 ingredients. Mix.

**Oriental Dressing:** Mix all 7 ingredients in small bowl. Makes ½ cup (125 mL) dressing. Pour over salad. Toss. Makes 10 cups (2.5 L), enough for 10 servings.

*1 serving: 103 Calories; 1.6 g Total Fat; 146 mg Sodium; 3 g Protein; 19 g Carbohydrate; 2 g Dietary Fiber*

# CHICKEN PASTA SALAD

*A good mixture. Cucumber adds a nice flavor and some crunch as well. Mild.*

| | | |
|---|---|---|
| Wagon wheels pasta | 8 oz. | 250 g |
| Boiling water | 2½ qts. | 2.5 L |
| Cooking oil (optional) | 1 tbsp. | 15 mL |
| Salt | 2 tsp. | 10 mL |
| Cooked peas | 2 cups | 500 mL |
| Cooked chicken, diced | 1 cup | 250 mL |
| Peeled, seeded and diced cucumber | ½ cup | 125 mL |
| **DRESSING** | | |
| Light salad dressing (or mayonnaise) | ½ cup | 125 mL |
| White vinegar | 1 tsp. | 5 mL |
| Seasoned salt | ¾ tsp. | 4 mL |

Cook pasta in boiling water, cooking oil and salt in large uncovered pot or Dutch oven for 5 to 7 minutes, stirring occasionally, until tender but firm. Drain. Rinse with cold water. Drain well. Turn pasta into large bowl.

Add peas, chicken and cucumber. Mix.

**Dressing:** Mix all 3 ingredients in small bowl. Add to pasta mixture. Toss to coat. Makes 6⅔ cups (1.65 L), enough for 6 servings.

*1 serving: 274 Calories; 6.3 g Total Fat; 320 mg Sodium; 15 g Protein; 39 g Carbohydrate; 4 g Dietary Fiber*

## MACARONI SALAD

*Make this in the morning to allow flavors to meld.*

| | | |
|---|---|---|
| Elbow macaroni | 2 cups | 500 mL |
| Chopped onion | ½ cup | 125 mL |
| Boiling water | 3 qts. | 3 L |
| Cooking oil (optional) | 1 tbsp. | 15 mL |
| Salt | 2 tsp. | 10 mL |
| Can of mixed vegetables, drained | 14 oz. | 398 mL |
| Chopped celery | ½ cup | 125 mL |
| Chopped green pepper | ⅓ cup | 75 mL |
| Chopped pimiento | 2 tbsp. | 30 mL |
| **DRESSING** | | |
| Light salad dressing (or mayonnaise) | ¾ cup | 175 mL |
| Milk | ¼ cup | 60 mL |
| Prepared mustard | 1 tsp. | 5 mL |
| Granulated sugar | 1 tsp. | 5 mL |
| Salt | ½ tsp. | 2 mL |
| Pepper | ¼ tsp. | 1 mL |

Cook macaroni and onion in boiling water, cooking oil and salt in large uncovered pot or Dutch oven for 5 to 7 minutes, stirring occasionally, until tender but firm. Drain. Rinse with cold water. Drain well. Turn macaroni into large bowl.

Add next 4 ingredients.

**Dressing:** Mix all 6 ingredients in small bowl. Pour over pasta mixture. Toss. Makes 6½ cups (1.6 L), enough for 6 servings.

*1 serving: 241 Calories; 8.2 g Total Fat; 506 mg Sodium; 6 g Protein; 36 g Carbohydrate; 2 g Dietary Fiber*

## SHRIMP PASTA SALAD

*Tomato and shrimp make this salad both a pleasure to the eye and the taste buds.*

| | | |
|---|---|---|
| Rotini pasta | 2⅔ cups | 650 mL |
| Boiling water | 3 qts. | 3 L |
| Cooking oil (optional) | 2 tsp. | 10 mL |
| Salt | 2 tsp. | 10 mL |
| Large hard-boiled eggs, chopped | 2 | 2 |
| Can of cocktail shrimp, drained and rinsed | 4 oz. | 113 g |
| Chopped celery | ½ cup | 125 mL |
| Green onions, chopped | 2 | 2 |
| Medium tomato, diced | 1 | 1 |
| Light salad dressing (or mayonnaise) | ⅓ cup | 75 mL |
| Non-fat sour cream | 2 tbsp. | 30 mL |
| Granulated sugar | ½ tsp. | 2 mL |
| Onion powder | ⅛ tsp. | 0.5 mL |
| Salt | ¼ tsp. | 1 mL |

Cook pasta in boiling water, cooking oil and first amount of salt in large uncovered pot or Dutch oven for 10 to 12 minutes, stirring occasionally, until tender but firm. Drain. Rinse with cold water. Drain well. Turn pasta into large bowl.

Add next 5 ingredients. Mix.

Mix remaining 5 ingredients in small bowl. Add to pasta mixture. Stir. Makes 6½ cups (1.6 L), enough for 6 servings.

*1 serving: 219 Calories; 5.8 g Total Fat; 262 mg Sodium; 10 g Protein; 31 g Carbohydrate; 1 g Dietary Fiber*

# CRAB SEAFOOD SALAD

*Easy to make. Serve in a lettuce cup for added color.*

| | | |
|---|---|---|
| Tiny shell pasta | 2 cups | 500 mL |
| Boiling water | 3 qts. | 3 L |
| Cooking oil (optional) | 1 tbsp. | 15 mL |
| Salt | 2 tsp. | 10 mL |
| Light salad dressing (or mayonnaise) | ¾ cup | 175 mL |
| Chili sauce | 1 tbsp. | 15 mL |
| Lemon juice | 1 tsp. | 5 mL |
| Worcestershire sauce | ½ tsp. | 2 mL |
| Onion powder | ¼ tsp. | 1 mL |
| Salt | ¼ tsp. | 1 mL |
| Can of crabmeat, drained, cartilage removed, flaked | 4½ oz. | 120 g |
| Chopped fresh parsley | ¼ cup | 60 mL |
| Paprika, sprinkle | | |

Cook pasta in boiling water, cooking oil and first amount of salt in large uncovered pot or Dutch oven for 8 to 11 minutes, stirring occasionally, until tender but firm. Drain. Rinse with cold water. Drain well. Turn pasta into large bowl.

Combine salad dressing, chili sauce, lemon juice, Worcestershire sauce, onion powder and second amount of salt in small bowl. Stir. Pour over pasta. Toss well.

Add crabmeat and parsley. Toss lightly. Sprinkle with paprika. Makes about 3¼ cups (800 mL), enough for 4 servings.

*1 serving:* 422 Calories; 15.9 g Total Fat; 965 mg Sodium; 13 g Protein; 56 g Carbohydrate; 2 g Dietary Fiber

# PESTO-SAUCED SALAD

*Pesto (PEH-stoh) is a rich sauce made from fresh sweet basil. It is available in supermarkets and Italian stores. A real Italian salad.*

| | | |
|---|---|---|
| Fusilli (spiral) pasta | 1 lb. | 454 g |
| Boiling water | 4 qts. | 4 L |
| Cooking oil (optional) | 1 tbsp. | 15 mL |
| Salt | 4 tsp. | 20 mL |
| Broccoli, cut up and cooked tender-crisp | 2 cups | 500 mL |
| Cauliflower, cut up and cooked tender-crisp | 2 cups | 500 mL |
| Pea pods, cooked tender-crisp | 2 cups | 500 mL |
| Sliced carrot, cooked tender-crisp | 1½ cups | 375 mL |
| Sliced fresh mushrooms | 1 cup | 250 mL |
| **PESTO DRESSING** | | |
| Basil pesto | ¾ cup | 175 mL |
| White vinegar | ⅓ cup | 75 mL |
| Olive oil | ⅔ cup | 150 mL |
| Grated Parmesan cheese | ½ cup | 125 mL |
| Salt | 1 tsp. | 5 mL |

Cook pasta in boiling water, cooking oil and salt in large uncovered pot or Dutch oven for 8 to 10 minutes, stirring occasionally, until tender but firm. Drain well. Rinse with cold water. Drain. Turn into large bowl.

Add broccoli, cauliflower, pea pods, carrot and mushrooms. Stir.

**Pesto Dressing:** Mix all 5 ingredients in small bowl. Pour over pasta mixture. Toss to coat. Serves 8.

*1 serving:* 529 Calories; 29.5 g Total Fat; 501 mg Sodium; 14 g Protein; 54 g Carbohydrate; 5 g Dietary Fiber

# Potato Salads

The humble potato, dressed up in one of these salad recipes, is certain to become the most popular vegetable at the picnic. It's high time we turned that potato into something spectacular—spruce it up in Sweet Potato Salad, page 44, or try Hot Potato Salad, page 42, as a side dish to roast beef. Everyone will applaud the change!

## CRUNCHY POTATO SALAD

*Very colorful. Watch the cooking time of the potato as it will differ depending on its size.*

| | | |
|---|---|---|
| Unpeeled large potato, cut crosswise into 3 pieces | 1 | 1 |
| Water | 1 cup | 250 mL |
| Salt | ¼ tsp. | 1 mL |
| Diced red pepper | 2 tbsp. | 30 mL |
| Grated carrot | 1 tbsp. | 15 mL |
| Finely diced celery | 1 tbsp. | 15 mL |
| Sliced green onion | 1 tbsp. | 15 mL |
| Grated Cheddar cheese | 2 tbsp. | 30 mL |
| Light Italian dressing | 2 tbsp. | 30 mL |
| Salt, sprinkle | | |
| Pepper, sprinkle | | |

Put potato pieces, water and salt into small saucepan. Bring to a boil. Cover. Simmer for about 13 minutes until potato is tender. Drain. Cool slightly. Dice into small cubes.

Combine potato and remaining 8 ingredients in small bowl. Stir. Chill until cold. Makes 1½ cups (375 mL), enough for 2 large servings.

*1 serving:* 158 Calories; 3.9 g Total Fat; 358 mg Sodium; 5 g Protein; 27 g Carbohydrate; 2 g Dietary Fiber

## HOT POTATO SALAD

*A good and different way to serve potatoes. Dressing has just the right tang.*

| | | |
|---|---|---|
| **Medium potatoes** | 4 | 4 |
| **Bacon slices, diced** | 4 | 4 |
| **Chopped onion** | ½ cup | 125 mL |
| **All-purpose flour** | 1 tbsp. | 15 mL |
| **Salt** | 1 tsp. | 5 mL |
| **Pepper** | ⅛ tsp. | 0.5 mL |
| **Beef bouillon powder** | 1 tsp. | 5 mL |
| **White vinegar** | 2 tbsp. | 30 mL |
| **Water** | ¼ cup | 60 mL |
| **Light salad dressing (or mayonnaise)** | ¼ cup | 60 mL |
| **Granulated sugar** | 1 tbsp. | 15 mL |

Prick each potato in 3 or 4 places. Arrange in circle in microwave. Microwave, uncovered, on high (100%) for about 6 minutes. Turn potatoes over. Rearrange potatoes in microwave if you don't have a turntable. Microwave on high (100%) for about 5 minutes. Test with sharp knife. Microwave and test at 1 minute intervals until almost cooked. Let stand, covered with foil to keep warm, for 5 minutes.

Combine bacon and onion in small microwave-safe bowl. Cover. Microwave on high (100%) for about 2 minutes. Stir. Microwave, covered, on high (100%) for about 2 minutes. Stir every 30 seconds. Microwave on high (100%) until bacon is cooked and onion is soft.

Mix in flour, salt, pepper and bouillon powder.

Stir in vinegar, water, salad dressing and sugar. Cover. Microwave on high (100%) for about 1 minute. Stir. Microwave on high (100%) for 1½ to 2 minutes until mixture is boiling and thickened. Peel potatoes. Cut into bite-size pieces. Place in serving bowl. Pour bacon mixture over top. Toss. Serves 4.

*1 serving:* 312 Calories; 17.3 g Total Fat; 1124 mg Sodium; 6 g Protein; 34 g Carbohydrate; 3 g Dietary Fiber

## POTATO RAITA

*Pronounced RI-tah. This potato salad has a different taste than most. The yogurt, ginger paste and coriander give this its East Indian flavor.*

| | | |
|---|---|---|
| **Plain yogurt** | ½ cup | 125 mL |
| **Lemon juice** | 1 tsp. | 5 mL |
| **Granulated sugar** | ½ tsp. | 2 mL |
| **Salt** | ½ tsp. | 2 mL |
| **Ginger paste** | ¼ tsp. | 1 mL |
| **Chopped fresh cilantro (coriander)** | 1 tbsp. | 15 mL |
| **Cold cubed cooked potato** | 4 cups | 1 L |

Mix first 6 ingredients in small bowl. Stir well.

Add to potato in large bowl. Mix. Makes about 4 cups (1 L), enough for 4 servings.

*1 serving:* 141 Calories; 0.6 g Total Fat; 368 mg Sodium; 4 g Protein; 30 g Carbohydrate; 2 g Dietary Fiber

# POTATO SALAD

*Mix and let stand for at least one hour in the refrigerator to blend flavors. Colorful. Full of vegetables.*

| | | |
|---|---|---|
| Cold cubed cooked potato | 4 cups | 1 L |
| Large hard-boiled eggs, chopped | 4 | 4 |
| Grated carrot | ½ cup | 125 mL |
| Chopped celery | ½ cup | 125 mL |
| Green onions, sliced | 3 | 3 |
| Light salad dressing (or mayonnaise) | ½ cup | 125 mL |
| Sweet pickle relish | 2 tbsp. | 30 mL |
| Salt | ½ tsp. | 2 mL |
| Pepper | ⅛ tsp. | 0.5 mL |
| Milk, to thin | 3 tbsp. | 50 mL |
| Cherry tomatoes, quartered | 6 | 6 |

Combine first 5 ingredients in large bowl. Chill.

Mix next 5 ingredients in small bowl. Reserve 1 tbsp. (15 mL). Add remaining dressing to potato mixture. Toss well. Spoon into serving bowl.

Spread tomato pieces over top. Drizzle tomato with reserved dressing. Chill until ready to serve. Makes 6 cups (1.5 L), enough for 6 servings.

*1 serving: 220 Calories; 9.1 g Total Fat; 470 mg Sodium; 7 g Protein; 28 g Carbohydrate; 2 g Dietary Fiber*

Pictured on page 53.

# HOT POTATO SALAD

*Young or waxy potatoes work best with this, although any will do.*

| | | |
|---|---|---|
| Unpeeled medium whole potatoes | 8 | 8 |
| Boiling water, to cover | | |
| Salt | 1 tsp. | 5 mL |
| Bacon slices, diced | 10 | 10 |
| Chopped onion | 1 cup | 250 mL |
| Chopped celery | ½ cup | 125 mL |
| All-purpose flour | 2 tbsp. | 30 mL |
| Salt | 1 tsp. | 5 mL |
| Pepper | ¼ tsp. | 1 mL |
| Granulated sugar | 2 tbsp. | 30 mL |
| Water | ⅔ cup | 150 mL |
| White vinegar | ¼ cup | 60 mL |

Cook potatoes in boiling water and first amount of salt in medium saucepan until tender.

Combine bacon, onion and celery in frying pan. Sauté just until cooked.

Add flour, second amount of salt, pepper and sugar. Mix well. Stir in water and vinegar. Drain potatoes. Peel. Dice into large bowl. Add bacon mixture. Toss. Drizzle with more vinegar. Toss again if you would like a bit more zing. Serves 8.

*1 serving: 306 Calories; 16.5 g Total Fat; 559 mg Sodium; 6 g Protein; 35 g Carbohydrate; 3 g Dietary Fiber*

*Potato, macaroni and bean salads have been traditionally made with salad dressing or mayonnaise. Enjoy fresh new flavor and lower calories by using half non-fat sour cream and half light salad dressing or mayonnaise.*

## GERMAN POTATO SALAD

*Best to serve this warm. Nice change from the usual cold potato salad.*

| | | |
|---|---|---|
| Bacon slices | 6 | 6 |
| Small onion, finely chopped | 1 | 1 |
| All-purpose flour | 2 tbsp. | 30 mL |
| White vinegar | ¼ cup | 60 mL |
| Water | ¾ cup | 175 mL |
| Granulated sugar | 2 tbsp. | 30 mL |
| Parsley flakes | 1 tsp. | 5 mL |
| Salt | ½ tsp. | 2 mL |
| Pepper | ⅛ tsp. | 0.5 mL |
| Hot cooked cubed or sliced potato | 6 cups | 1.5 L |

Cook bacon in medium frying pan until crisp. Remove. Crumble. Set aside.

Slowly sauté onion in bacon fat until soft and clear. Stir in flour. Add vinegar and water. Stir until thickened. Stir in sugar, parsley, salt and pepper. Add bacon. Stir.

Pour bacon mixture over cubed potato. Toss and serve. Serves 6.

*1 serving: 204 Calories; 3.3 g Total Fat; 336 mg Sodium; 5 g Protein; 39 g Carbohydrate; 3 g Dietary Fiber*

## HOT ITALIAN SALAD

*This is served warm. A great way to bring the memory of summer potato salads into a winter meal. Uses leftover potato.*

| | | |
|---|---|---|
| Bacon slices | 6 | 6 |
| Cold cubed cooked potato | 4 cups | 1 L |
| Light Italian dressing | ½ cup | 125 mL |
| Green onions, sliced | 4-6 | 4-6 |
| Chopped celery | ½ cup | 125 mL |
| Grated Parmesan cheese | ½ cup | 125 mL |

Fry bacon in frying pan until crisp. Remove. Crumble. Drain. Return bacon to frying pan.

Add potato, dressing, green onion and celery. Stir to heat through.

Spoon into serving bowl. Add cheese. Stir. Serves 4.

*1 serving: 280 Calories; 10.4 g Total Fat; 1135 mg Sodium; 12 g Protein; 36 g Carbohydrate; 3 g Dietary Fiber*

## SWEET POTATO SALAD

*Now this is really different! It will be a hit at the next summer barbecue.*

| | | |
|---|---|---|
| Cooking oil | 2 tbsp. | 30 mL |
| Reserved pineapple juice | 2 tbsp. | 30 mL |
| Lemon juice | 1 tbsp. | 15 mL |
| Salt | ½ tsp. | 2 mL |
| Onion salt | ¼ tsp. | 1 mL |
| Cold cubed cooked sweet potato | 3 cups | 750 mL |
| Can of pineapple tidbits, drained and juice reserved | 14 oz. | 398 mL |
| Chopped celery | ¾ cup | 175 mL |
| Slivered almonds | ¼ cup | 60 mL |

Combine cooking oil, reserved pineapple juice and lemon juice in medium bowl. Add both salts. Add sweet potato. Stir. Marinate for about 1 hour.

Add pineapple, celery and almonds. Toss lightly. Serves 10.

*1 serving: 157 Calories; 4.9 g Total Fat; 190 mg Sodium; 2 g Protein; 27 g Carbohydrate; 3 g Dietary Fiber*

# Rice Salads

ice is an international favorite ingredient—and many varieties of rice are quickly gaining popularity as they become more readily available. Sample some of these great recipes, like Tabbouleh, page 46, and discover what countries all over the world already know—rice is a perfect side dish to any food!

## RICE ARTICHOKE SALAD

*Creamy salad. Flecks of color throughout. Make rice two or three days in advance. Keep chilled. Cut up vegetables the night before serving. Make dressing and assemble salad in the morning.*

| | | |
|---|---|---|
| Long grain white rice | 1 cup | 250 mL |
| Water | 2 cups | 500 mL |
| Chicken bouillon powder | 1 tbsp. | 15 mL |
| Small green pepper, chopped | 1 | 1 |
| Sliced green onion | ¼ cup | 60 mL |
| Sliced radish | ¼ cup | 60 mL |
| Jars of marinated artichoke hearts (6 oz., 170 mL, each), drained | 2 | 2 |
| **DRESSING** | | |
| Light salad dressing (or mayonnaise) | ⅓ cup | 75 mL |
| Milk | 1 tbsp. | 15 mL |
| Curry powder (or more to taste) | ¼ tsp. | 1 mL |

Cook rice slowly in water and bouillon powder in small saucepan for about 15 minutes until rice is tender and liquid is absorbed. Cool.

Add next 4 ingredients. Stir together.

**Dressing:** Mix salad dressing, milk and curry powder in medium bowl. Add to rice mixture. Stir. Makes 6 cups (1.5 L), enough for 8 servings.

*1 serving: 141 Calories; 3.1 g Total Fat; 415 mg Sodium; 3 g Protein; 25 g Carbohydrate; 6 g Dietary Fiber*

## TABBOULEH

*Bulgur consists of wheat kernels that have been steamed, dried and crushed.*

| | | |
|---|---|---|
| Bulgur | 1 cup | 250 mL |
| Boiling water | 1 cup | 250 mL |
| Medium roma (plum) tomatoes, diced | 2 | 2 |
| Thinly sliced red onion | ½ cup | 125 mL |
| Medium green or yellow pepper, diced | ½ | ½ |
| Thinly sliced green onion | ¼ cup | 60 mL |
| Chopped fresh mint leaves | ⅓ cup | 75 mL |
| Chopped fresh parsley | ½ cup | 125 mL |
| **LEMON DRESSING** | | |
| Lemon juice | ¼ cup | 60 mL |
| Garlic clove, minced | 1 | 1 |
| Lemon pepper | ½ tsp. | 2 mL |
| Olive oil | 1 tbsp. | 15 mL |
| Apple juice | ¼ cup | 60 mL |
| Salt | ¼ tsp. | 1 mL |

Place bulgur in medium bowl. Pour boiling water over. Stir. Let stand for 30 minutes until water is absorbed.

Add next 6 ingredients. Mix well.

**Lemon Dressing:** Combine all 6 ingredients in small bowl. Stir. Pour over bulgur mixture. Stir. Cover. Chill for at least 2 hours. Makes 4½ cups (1.1 L), enough for 6 servings.

*1 serving:* 132 Calories; 2.8 g Total Fat; 125 mg Sodium; 4 g Protein; 25 g Carbohydrate; 6 g Dietary Fiber

Pictured on page 54.

## RICE AND BEAN SALAD

*Makes lots of colorful salad.*

| | | |
|---|---|---|
| Long grain white rice | 1¼ cups | 300 mL |
| Chopped onion | ½ cup | 125 mL |
| Boiling water | 2½ cups | 625 mL |
| Frozen kernel corn, thawed | 1¼ cups | 300 mL |
| Can of kidney beans, drained | 14 oz. | 398 mL |
| Chopped green onion | ¼ cup | 60 mL |
| Large tomato, seeded and diced | 1 | 1 |
| Light Italian dressing | 1 cup | 250 mL |
| Chili powder | 1 tsp. | 5 mL |

Combine rice and onion in boiling water in medium saucepan. Cover. Simmer for 15 to 20 minutes until rice is tender and water is absorbed. Cool.

Combine corn, kidney beans, green onion and tomato in large bowl. Add rice mixture. Stir together.

Add Italian dressing. Sprinkle with chili powder. Stir well. Makes 9 cups (2.25 L), enough for 6 servings.

*1 serving:* 258 Calories; 2.2 g Total Fat; 696 mg Sodium; 8 g Protein; 53 g Carbohydrate; 5 g Dietary Fiber

*For a fluffier, less sticky rice, measure uncooked rice into colander. Rinse with water several times. Converted rice will also result in a softer, fluffier rice.*

# SHRIMPY RICE SALAD

*This is a beautiful platter presentation for a buffet. Cook rice the day before. Prepare and add vegetables and shrimp to rice in the morning. Cover and chill. Also prepare lettuce, tomatoes and dressing in the morning. Cover and chill each separately. Assemble salad just before serving.*

| | | |
|---|---|---|
| Long grain white rice | 1 cup | 250 mL |
| Boiling water | 2 cups | 500 mL |
| Sliced pimiento-stuffed olives | ½ cup | 125 mL |
| Chopped celery | ⅓ cup | 75 mL |
| Slivered or chopped green pepper | ¼ cup | 60 mL |
| Chopped pimiento | ¼ cup | 60 mL |
| Finely chopped red onion | ¼ cup | 60 mL |
| Cooked shrimp (or crabmeat), canned, fresh or frozen, thawed | 1 cup | 250 mL |
| Light salad dressing (or mayonnaise) | 3 tbsp. | 50 mL |
| Milk | 1 tbsp. | 15 mL |
| Lemon juice | 1 tsp. | 5 mL |
| Salt | ½ tsp. | 2 mL |
| Pepper | ½ tsp. | 2 mL |
| Shredded iceberg lettuce, lightly packed | 4 cups | 1 L |
| Medium tomatoes, each cut into 8 wedges | 2 | 2 |
| French dressing | ½ cup | 125 mL |

Cook rice in boiling water in small saucepan for about 15 minutes until rice is tender and liquid is absorbed. Turn into large bowl. Cool.

Add next 6 ingredients. Stir.

Mix salad dressing, milk, lemon juice, salt and pepper in small bowl. Add to rice mixture. Stir well.

Spread lettuce on platter. Spoon salad mixture in center almost to edge. Arrange tomato wedges around outside edge. Drizzle French dressing over just before serving. Makes 8½ cups (2.1 L), enough for 8 generous servings.

*1 serving:  207 Calories; 9.4 g Total Fat; 707 mg Sodium; 6 g Protein; 25 g Carbohydrate; 2 g Dietary Fiber*

# RICE SALAD

*This salad can also be stuffed into a pita bread for a salad sandwich.*

| | | |
|---|---|---|
| Cooked white rice | ¾ cup | 175 mL |
| Cooked ham, chopped | 2 oz. | 57 g |
| Sliced green onion | 2 tbsp. | 30 mL |
| Cooked vegetables (such as peas, broccoli florets or green beans) | ½ cup | 125 mL |
| Grated carrot | ¼ cup | 60 mL |
| Olive oil | 1 tsp. | 5 mL |
| White (or wine or apple cider) vinegar | 2 tsp. | 10 mL |
| Salt, sprinkle | | |

Combine all 8 ingredients in small bowl. Mix well. Makes 1½ cups (375 mL), enough for 1 generous serving.

*1 serving: 272 Calories; 7.5 g Total Fat; 508 mg Sodium; 12 g Protein; 39 g Carbohydrate; 3 g Dietary Fiber*

Pictured on page 35 and back cover.

**Variation:** Add 2 tbsp. (30 mL) sunflower seeds or pumpkin seeds, or add ¼ cup (60 mL) raisins.

# Tossed Salads

**W**ith all the varieties of ingredients and salad dressings available today, no one can say that a tossed salad is boring. It's classic, colorful, versatile and best of all, simple. Try Spring Salad, page 50, when family and friends next gather, and they will be impressed with the piquant flavors and colorful presentation.

## WALDORF SPINACH TOSS

*Combine two old favorites for a new holiday salad.*

| | | |
|---|---|---|
| Toasted pecan pieces, optional (see Tip, page 21) | ³⁄₄ cup | 175 mL |
| Medium red apple, with peel, cored and sliced into thin wedges | 1 | 1 |
| Medium orange, peeled (white pith removed), halved and thinly sliced | 1 | 1 |
| Red onion, thinly sliced and separated | ¹⁄₂ cup | 125 mL |
| Bags of fresh spinach (10 oz., 285 g, each), torn bite size | 2 | 2 |
| **DRESSING** | | |
| Granulated sugar | ¹⁄₄ cup | 60 mL |
| Dry mustard | ¹⁄₂ tsp. | 2 mL |
| Hot pepper sauce | ¹⁄₁₆ tsp. | 0.5 mL |
| White vinegar | ¹⁄₄ cup | 60 mL |
| Cooking oil | ¹⁄₄ cup | 60 mL |

Reserve ¹⁄₄ cup (60 mL) pecans for dressing. Place pecans, apple, orange, red onion and spinach in large bowl.

**Dressing:** Combine reserved pecans, sugar, mustard, hot pepper sauce, vinegar and cooking oil in blender. Process for 2 minutes until smooth. Pour over spinach mixture. Toss to coat salad. Serves 6 to 8.

*1 serving: 260 Calories; 10.1 g Total Fat; 76 mg Sodium; 3 g Protein; 20 g Carbohydrate; 5 g Dietary Fiber*

Pictured on page 36.

# TRADITIONAL CAESAR

*A variation of the traditional garlic-flavored dressing is used with this salad.*

| | | |
|---|---|---|
| Head of romaine lettuce, torn | 1 | 1 |
| Herb or plain croutons | ½ cup | 125 mL |
| Grated Parmesan cheese | 2 tbsp. | 30 mL |
| Cooked and crumbled bacon | ¼ cup | 60 mL |
| Creamy Garlic Dressing, page 9 | ⅓ cup | 75 mL |
| Grated Parmesan cheese, sprinkle | | |

Toss first 4 ingredients together in large bowl.

Add dressing when ready to serve. Toss.

Sprinkle with Parmesan cheese. Serves 6.

*1 serving: 86 Calories; 5.3 g Total Fat; 228 mg Sodium; 4 g Protein; 6 g Carbohydrate; 1 g Dietary Fiber*

**CHICKEN CAESAR SALAD:** Fry 1 boneless, skinless chicken breast half for each serving. Place on plate beside salad, or sliver or slice chicken and place on top of salad. Add chicken while hot.

*To keep hard cheese from becoming crusty, rub a bit of butter or cooking oil on the crusty area and rewrap.*

# CAESAR SALAD

*Another variation of a great salad.*

**DRESSING**

| | | |
|---|---|---|
| Cooking oil | ⅓ cup | 75 mL |
| Medium garlic clove, quartered | 1 | 1 |
| Large egg | 1 | 1 |
| Apple cider vinegar | 2 tbsp. | 30 mL |
| Lemon juice | 1 tbsp. | 15 mL |
| Salt | ¼ tsp. | 1 mL |
| Pepper | ¼ tsp. | 1 mL |
| Anchovy paste | 2 tsp. | 10 mL |
| Grated Parmesan cheese | ½ cup | 125 mL |
| Medium head of romaine lettuce | 1 | 1 |
| Small head of iceberg lettuce | 1 | 1 |
| Seasoned Croutons, page 8 | 2 cups | 500 mL |

**Dressing:** Combine cooking oil and garlic in small bowl. Let stand overnight or for at least a few hours. Remove garlic. Either discard or chop it finely to add a stronger garlic flavor.

Add next 7 ingredients. Stir well. Makes about 1 cup (250 mL) dressing.

Tear salad greens into bite-size pieces into large bowl. Add dressing and croutons. Toss well. Serves 8 generously.

*1 serving: 237 Calories; 19.2 g Total Fat; 432 mg Sodium; 7 g Protein; 10 g Carbohydrate; 2 g Dietary Fiber*

## SPRING SALAD

*A different dressing turns this into a light refreshing salad.*

**DRESSING**

| | | |
|---|---|---|
| Red wine vinegar | 1 tbsp. | 15 mL |
| Granulated sugar | 1 tbsp. | 15 mL |
| Cooking oil | 2 tbsp. | 30 mL |
| Dry mustard | ¼ tsp. | 1 mL |
| Torn assorted salad greens, lightly packed | 4 cups | 1 L |
| Chopped chives | 1 tbsp. | 15 mL |
| Seedless grapes, halved or whole | 1 cup | 250 mL |
| Grated medium Cheddar cheese | ½ cup | 125 mL |

**Dressing:** Mix first 4 ingredients in small bowl.

Combine remaining 4 ingredients in large bowl. Pour dressing over all. Toss. Serves 4.

*1 serving: 160 Calories; 12.2 g Total Fat; 108 mg Sodium; 5 g Protein; 9 g Carbohydrate; 1 g Dietary Fiber*

## POPPY SEED SALAD

*Have dressing made ahead and waiting in the refrigerator. Toss together at the last minute.*

**DRESSING**

| | | |
|---|---|---|
| Granulated sugar | ½ cup | 125 mL |
| White vinegar | 6 tbsp. | 100 mL |
| Cooking oil | 2½ tbsp. | 37 mL |
| Onion flakes | 1 tsp. | 5 mL |
| Dry mustard | ½ tsp. | 2 mL |
| Salt | ½ tsp. | 2 mL |
| Paprika | ¼ tsp. | 1 mL |
| Poppy seeds | 2½ tsp. | 12 mL |

| | | |
|---|---|---|
| Chopped iceberg lettuce, lightly packed | 8 cups | 2 L |
| Green onions, sliced | 3 | 3 |
| Radishes, sliced | 8 | 8 |
| Green pepper strips | ⅓ cup | 75 mL |

**Dressing:** Measure first 8 ingredients into small bowl. Beat well. Chill overnight. Makes ⅔ cup (150 mL) dressing.

Combine remaining 4 ingredients in large bowl. Pour dressing over top. Toss well. Serves 8.

*1 serving: 108 Calories; 4.9 g Total Fat; 178 mg Sodium; 1 g Protein; 16 g Carbohydrate; 1 g Dietary Fiber*

## SPINACH MUSHROOM SALAD

*Salad and dressing can be made ahead of time and tossed together at the last minute. Dressing is tangy.*

| | | |
|---|---|---|
| Bag of fresh spinach | 10 oz. | 285 g |
| Sliced fresh mushrooms | 2 cups | 500 mL |
| Sliced green onion | ⅓ cup | 75 mL |
| Bacon slices, cooked crisp and crumbled | 6 | 6 |

**DRESSING**

| | | |
|---|---|---|
| Cooking oil | 2 tbsp. | 30 mL |
| Lemon juice | 2 tbsp. | 30 mL |
| Egg yolk (large) | 1 | 1 |
| Salt | ¾ tsp. | 4 mL |
| Pepper | ⅛ tsp. | 0.5 mL |
| Granulated sugar | ½ tsp. | 2 mL |

Combine first 4 ingredients in large bowl. Cover. Chill until ready to serve.

**Dressing:** Stir all 6 ingredients in small bowl. Pour over spinach mixture. Toss to coat. Serves 8.

*1 serving: 84 Calories; 6.7 g Total Fat; 372 mg Sodium; 4 g Protein; 4 g Carbohydrate; 2 g Dietary Fiber*

# SPINACH TOMATO SALAD

*Very colorful with a just-the-right-nip dressing.*

**DRESSING**

| | | |
|---|---|---|
| Salad dressing (or mayonnaise) | 1 tbsp. | 15 mL |
| Cooking oil | 1½ tsp. | 7 mL |
| Red wine vinegar | 1½ tsp. | 7 mL |
| Granulated sugar | ½ tsp. | 2 mL |
| Salt | ⅛ tsp. | 0.5 mL |
| Pepper, sprinkle | | |
| Garlic powder, light sprinkle | | |
| | | |
| Bag of fresh spinach | 10 oz. | 285 g |
| Sliced fresh mushrooms | ¼ cup | 60 mL |
| Cherry tomatoes, quartered | 2 | 2 |
| | | |
| Large hard-boiled egg | 1 | 1 |
| Grated Parmesan cheese, sprinkle | | |

**Dressing:** Mix first 7 ingredients well in small bowl. Makes a scant 2 tbsp. (30 mL) dressing.

Put spinach, mushrooms and tomato pieces into large bowl. Add ¾ of dressing. Toss lightly and arrange on 2 individual salad plates. Have a few tomato pieces showing on top.

Cut egg in half lengthwise. With clean sharp knife cut each half into 3 long wedges. Divide between plates placing alongside spinach. Drizzle remaining dressing over all. Sprinkle with Parmesan cheese. Serves 2.

*1 serving: 120 Calories; 9.7 g Total Fat; 279 mg Sodium; 4 g Protein; 4 g Carbohydrate; 1 g Dietary Fiber*

# WILTED SPINACH

*Serve as a side salad or serve 4 for lunch.*

| | | |
|---|---|---|
| Torn spinach leaves, lightly packed | 6 cups | 1.5 L |
| Sliced fresh mushrooms | 1 cup | 250 mL |
| Finely chopped red onion | 2 tbsp. | 30 mL |
| **DRESSING** | | |
| Bacon slices | 4 | 4 |
| | | |
| Brown sugar, packed | 3 tbsp. | 50 mL |
| White vinegar | 3 tbsp. | 50 mL |
| Salt | ¼ tsp. | 1 mL |

Combine spinach, mushrooms and red onion in large bowl. Cover. Chill until ready to serve.

**Dressing:** Lay bacon on paper towel on plate. Cover with second paper towel. Microwave on high (100%) for about 4 minutes until cooked, rotating plate ½ turn after 2 minutes if you don't have a turntable. Crumble bacon.

Put brown sugar, vinegar and salt into 2 cup (500 mL) measure. Add bacon. Heat dressing on high (100%) for about 1 minute or until it begins to boil just before serving. Stir. Pour over salad. Toss well and serve. Serves 8.

*1 serving: 51 Calories; 1.8 g Total Fat; 172 mg Sodium; 2 g Protein; 8 g Carbohydrate; 1 g Dietary Fiber*

## MIXED SALAD

*So fresh looking and appetizing. Greens are the main ingredient with prosciutto, celery, cheese and tomatoes added.*

| | | |
|---|---|---|
| Large head of romaine lettuce, torn | 1 | 1 |
| Medium tomatoes, halved, cut each half into 4 wedges | 2 | 2 |
| Sliced celery | 1½ cups | 375 mL |
| Provolone (or other mild smoked) cheese, diced | ½ cup | 125 mL |
| Prosciutto (or cooked ham), diced | ½ cup | 125 mL |
| Olive (or cooking) oil | ¼ cup | 60 mL |
| Salt, sprinkle | | |
| Red wine vinegar | 1 tbsp. | 15 mL |
| Lemon juice | 1 tbsp. | 15 mL |

Place romaine lettuce in salad bowl. Add tomato wedges, celery, cheese and prosciutto.

Pour olive oil over top. Toss to coat.

Sprinkle with salt. Toss. Add vinegar and lemon juice. Toss again. Serves 8.

*1 serving: 124 Calories; 10.1 g Total Fat; 227 mg Sodium; 5 g Protein; 4 g Carbohydrate; 2 g Dietary Fiber*

## CRABBY TOSS

*It's a toss-up whether or not to double it.*

| | | |
|---|---|---|
| Torn iceberg lettuce, lightly packed | 2 cups | 500 mL |
| Diced cucumber | ½ cup | 125 mL |
| Diced celery | ½ cup | 125 mL |
| Green onions, sliced | 2 | 2 |
| Can of crabmeat, drained and cartilage removed | 5 oz. | 142 g |
| Light salad dressing (or mayonnaise) | ½ cup | 125 mL |
| Ketchup | 1 tbsp. | 15 mL |
| Worcestershire sauce | 1 tbsp. | 15 mL |
| Lemon juice | 1 tsp. | 5 mL |
| Salt | ½ tsp. | 2 mL |
| Pepper | ¼ tsp. | 1 mL |

Combine first 5 ingredients in medium bowl.

Mix salad dressing and ketchup in small bowl. Add Worcestershire sauce, lemon juice, salt and pepper. Stir. Add to crabmeat. Toss. Serves 4.

*1 serving: 128 Calories; 8.3 g Total Fat; 914 mg Sodium; 6 g Protein; 8 g Carbohydrate; 1 g Dietary Fiber*

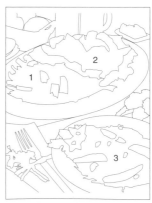

1. Pacific Rim Salad, page 24
2. Potato Salad, page 43
3. Bean Sprout Salad, page 62

Props Courtesy Of: Stokes, The Bay, X/S Wares

# VINAIGRETTE SALAD

*A tasty green mixture with red pimiento and yellow cheese added.*

| | | |
|---|---|---|
| Torn assorted salad greens, lightly packed | 8 cups | 2 L |
| Sliced celery | 1 cup | 250 mL |
| Chopped pimiento | 2-3 tbsp. | 30-45 mL |
| Grated medium Cheddar cheese | 1 cup | 250 mL |
| **DRESSING** | | |
| Cooking oil | 3 tbsp. | 50 mL |
| White vinegar | 3 tbsp. | 50 mL |
| Granulated sugar | 1 tbsp. | 15 mL |
| Salt | $\frac{1}{4}$ tsp. | 1 mL |
| Prepared mustard | 1 tsp. | 5 mL |

Combine first 4 ingredients in large bowl. Mix. Chill until shortly before needed.

**Dressing:** Measure all 5 ingredients into small bowl. Stir to blend. Pour over salad just before serving. Toss. Serves 8.

*1 serving:* 126 Calories; 10.3 g Total Fat; 216 mg Sodium; 5 g Protein; 4 g Carbohydrate; 1 g Dietary Fiber

# GREEN GODDESS SALAD

*A great addition to any meal. Makes a large salad. To reduce in size, use only part of the dressing on smaller quantity of lettuce.*

| | | |
|---|---|---|
| Medium heads of iceberg lettuce, torn | 2 | 2 |
| **DRESSING** | | |
| Light salad dressing (or mayonnaise) | 1 cup | 250 mL |
| Non-fat sour cream | $\frac{1}{2}$ cup | 125 mL |
| Chopped green onion | $\frac{1}{4}$ cup | 60 mL |
| Chopped fresh parsley | $\frac{1}{4}$ cup | 60 mL |
| Anchovy paste | 2 tsp. | 10 mL |
| Worcestershire sauce | 1 tsp. | 5 mL |
| Prepared mustard | $\frac{1}{2}$ tsp. | 2 mL |
| Salt | $\frac{1}{2}$ tsp. | 2 mL |
| Pepper | $\frac{1}{8}$ tsp. | 0.5 mL |
| Garlic powder (or 1 clove, minced) | $\frac{1}{4}$ tsp. | 1 mL |
| Cooked fresh crabmeat (or shrimp) | 1 cup | 250 mL |

Chill lettuce.

**Dressing:** Combine first 10 ingredients in medium bowl. Mix well. Makes 2 cups (500 mL) dressing.

Toss lettuce, dressing and crabmeat together in large bowl just before serving. Serves 8.

*1 serving:* 131 Calories; 8.5 g Total Fat; 632 mg Sodium; 5 g Protein; 9 g Carbohydrate; 2 g Dietary Fiber

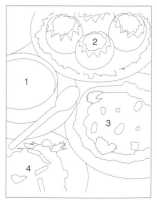

1. Cream Of Garlic Soup, page 97
2. Stuffed Tomato Salad, page 66
3. Tabbouleh, page 46
4. Bean Salad, page 62

Props Courtesy Of: C C On Whyle, The Bay, X/S Wares

## GREEK SALAD

*This can be assembled in a large bowl rather than individually. To increase tartness of dressing, simply add a bit more red wine vinegar.*

| | | |
|---|---|---|
| Head of romaine lettuce, torn | 1 | 1 |
| Medium tomatoes, cubed | 2 | 2 |
| Sliced cucumber | 1 cup | 250 mL |
| Slivered onion | 1 cup | 250 mL |
| Pitted ripe olives | 24 | 24 |
| Cubed or crumbled feta cheese | 1 cup | 250 mL |
| Medium green pepper, slivered | 1 | 1 |
| **RED WINE DRESSING** | | |
| Water | ½ cup | 125 mL |
| Cornstarch | 2 tsp. | 10 mL |
| Red wine vinegar | 3 tbsp. | 50 mL |
| Cooking oil | 1 tbsp. | 15 mL |
| Salt | ½ tsp. | 2 mL |
| Pepper | ⅛ tsp. | 0.5 mL |
| Dried whole oregano | ⅛ tsp. | 0.5 mL |
| Dried sweet basil | ⅛ tsp. | 0.5 mL |
| Garlic powder | ⅛ tsp. | 0.5 mL |
| Parsley flakes | 1 tsp. | 5 mL |

Divide lettuce among 8 individual large plates.

Divide next 6 ingredients equally over lettuce.

**Red Wine Dressing:** Measure water and cornstarch into small saucepan. Heat, stirring constantly, until boiling and thickened. Cool.

Combine remaining 8 ingredients in small bowl. Mix well. Add cooled cornstarch mixture. Stir together well. Makes ¾ cup (175 mL) dressing. Serve salad with dressing on the side. Serves 8.

*1 serving: 106 Calories; 7 g Total Fat; 468 mg Sodium; 4 g Protein; 8 g Carbohydrate; 2 g Dietary Fiber*

Pictured on page 107.

## SPRINGTIME SALAD

*Actually, delicious in all four seasons.*

| | | |
|---|---|---|
| Torn spinach (or romaine) leaves, lightly packed | 4 cups | 1 L |
| Medium red pepper, slivered | ½ | ½ |
| Small red onion, thinly sliced and separated into rings | ½ | ½ |
| Croutons, page 8 | ½ cup | 125 mL |
| Sunflower seeds | ¼ cup | 60 mL |
| Italian dressing | ⅓ cup | 75 mL |

Combine spinach, red pepper and red onion rings in large bowl. Cover. Chill.

Add croutons, sunflower seeds and dressing just before serving. Toss well. Serves 4.

*1 serving: 222 Calories; 19.4 g Total Fat; 410 mg Sodium; 5 g Protein; 10 g Carbohydrate; 3 g Dietary Fiber*

# MIXED SALAD

*An interesting mixture brought to life with a garlic, oil and vinegar dressing.*

**GARLIC DRESSING**

| | | |
|---|---|---|
| Cooking oil | ½ cup | 125 mL |
| White vinegar | ¼ cup | 60 mL |
| Granulated sugar | 1 tsp. | 5 mL |
| Garlic powder | ½ tsp. | 2 mL |
| Salt | 2 tsp. | 10 mL |
| Pepper | ½ tsp. | 2 mL |
| Dry mustard | ½ tsp. | 2 mL |

**SALAD**

| | | |
|---|---|---|
| Torn assorted salad greens, lightly packed | 3 cups | 750 mL |
| Grated medium Cheddar cheese | ½ cup | 125 mL |
| Medium avocado, peeled and cubed | 1 | 1 |
| Can of cut green (or kidney) beans, drained | 14 oz. | 398 mL |
| Medium tomato, cut up | 1 | 1 |
| Green onions, chopped | 2 | 2 |
| Croutons, page 8 | 1 cup | 250 mL |
| Corn chips, for garnish | 1 cup | 250 mL |

**Garlic Dressing:** Measure all 7 ingredients into small bowl. Stir together. Set aside. Makes ¾ cup (175 mL) dressing.

**Salad:** Combine first 6 ingredients in large bowl. Toss with dressing.

Sprinkle croutons and corn chips over top. Serves 8.

*1 serving:* 260 Calories; 24.2 g Total Fat; 860 mg Sodium; 4 g Protein; 9 g Carbohydrate; 2 g Dietary Fiber

Pictured on page 35 and back cover.

# TOSSED VEGGIE SALAD

*Colorfully loaded with vegetables.*

| | | |
|---|---|---|
| Torn assorted salad greens, lightly packed | 8 cups | 2 L |
| Small broccoli florets (see Note) | ½ cup | 125 mL |
| Small cauliflower florets (see Note) | ½ cup | 125 mL |
| Sliced fresh mushrooms | ½ cup | 125 mL |
| Diced tomato | ½ cup | 125 mL |
| Grated carrot | ½ cup | 125 mL |

**DRESSING**

| | | |
|---|---|---|
| Light salad dressing (or mayonnaise) | 1 cup | 250 mL |
| Ketchup | 1 tbsp. | 15 mL |
| Prepared mustard | 1 tsp. | 5 mL |
| Prepared horseradish | ½ tsp. | 2 mL |
| Milk | 2 tbsp. | 30 mL |

Combine first 6 ingredients in large bowl. Chill.

**Dressing:** Mix all 5 ingredients in small bowl. Add a bit more milk if too thick. Makes 1¼ cups (300 mL) dressing. Pour dressing over salad. Toss. Serves 8.

*1 serving:* 113 Calories; 8.2 g Total Fat; 298 mg Sodium; 2 g Protein; 9 g Carbohydrate; 2 g Dietary Fiber

**Note:** Parboiling the broccoli and cauliflower for 4 minutes will make them slightly tender as well as bring out the bright green color in the broccoli.

*To keep dressing clinging to lettuce, lettuce should be dry. Use a salad spinner, or turn a saucer upside down in a bowl and any leftover water will run out underneath.*

## Corn Chip Salad

*Crunchy with the taste of corn chips. Chili powder adds an extra touch along with the dressing.*

| | | |
|---|---|---|
| **Small head of iceberg lettuce, torn** | 1 | 1 |
| **Grated medium or sharp Cheddar cheese** | 2 cups | 500 mL |
| **Medium tomatoes, diced and drained on paper towel** | 2 | 2 |
| **Green onions, sliced** | 3-4 | 3-4 |
| **Can of ranch-style (or kidney) beans (14 oz., 398 mL), drained and rinsed** | ½ | ½ |
| **Chili powder** | 1 tsp. | 5 mL |
| **ISLAND DRESSING** | | |
| **Cooking oil** | 1 tbsp. | 15 mL |
| **All-purpose flour** | 1 tbsp. | 15 mL |
| **Water** | 3 tbsp. | 50 mL |
| **White vinegar** | 2 tbsp. | 30 mL |
| **Granulated sugar** | ¼ cup | 60 mL |
| **Ketchup** | 2 tsp. | 10 mL |
| **Onion powder** | ⅛ tsp. | 0.5 mL |
| **Salt** | ⅛ tsp. | 0.5 mL |
| **Corn chips** | 3 cups | 750 mL |

Combine first 6 ingredients in large bowl. Toss.

**Island Dressing:** Measure cooking oil and flour into small saucepan.

Stir in next 6 ingredients. Heat, stirring constantly, until mixture boils and thickens. Cool thoroughly before using. Makes ½ cup (125 mL) dressing. Add to salad. Toss well to coat. Chill for 30 minutes.

Add corn chips just before serving. Toss. Makes 10 cups (2.5 L), enough for 10 servings.

*1 serving: 267 Calories; 15.3 g Total Fat; 425 mg Sodium; 9 g Protein; 24 g Carbohydrate; 3 g Dietary Fiber*

## Creamy Greens

*Might look like Caesar Salad but dressed with a hint of blue cheese.*

| | | |
|---|---|---|
| **Small head of romaine lettuce (or assorted salad greens), torn** | 1 | 1 |
| **Green onions, sliced** | 2-3 | 2-3 |
| **Large hard-boiled eggs, sliced or chopped** | 2 | 2 |
| **Crumbled blue cheese (to taste)** | 2-4 tsp. | 10-20 mL |
| **Non-fat sour cream** | ¼ cup | 60 mL |
| **Light salad dressing (or mayonnaise)** | ¼ cup | 60 mL |
| **Milk** | 2 tbsp. | 30 mL |

Combine lettuce, green onion and egg in large bowl.

Mix remaining 4 ingredients in small bowl. Add to lettuce mixture. Toss. Serves 6.

*1 serving: 76 Calories; 5 g Total Fat; 132 mg Sodium; 4 g Protein; 4 g Carbohydrate; 1 g Dietary Fiber*

# Vegetable Salads

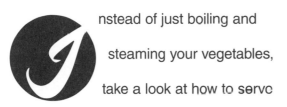

nstead of just boiling and steaming your vegetables, take a look at how to serve vegetables as part of a nutritious salad. Here are some exceptional recipes that offer you a wide choice of vegetable salads. Reluctant fans of cooked carrots might express more enthusiasm for the vegetable if served as Oriental Salad, page 63.

## SUPER SALAD

*Chill dressing and salad separately. Combine when ready to serve. A great starter salad.*

**SUPER DRESSING**

| | | |
|---|---|---|
| Cooking oil | 2 tbsp. | 30 mL |
| Red wine vinegar | 2 tbsp. | 30 mL |
| Dijon mustard | 1 tsp. | 5 mL |
| Dill weed | ½ tsp. | 2 mL |
| Garlic powder | ⅛ tsp. | 0.5 mL |
| Salt | ½ tsp. | 2 mL |
| Pepper | ½ tsp. | 2 mL |
| Small broccoli florets | 4 cups | 1 L |
| Water | ½ cup | 125 mL |
| Sliced fresh mushrooms | 2 cups | 500 mL |
| Frozen pea pods, thawed and drained | 6 oz. | 170 g |
| Toasted slivered or sliced almonds (see Tip, page 21) | ½ cup | 125 mL |
| Head of romaine lettuce, torn | 1 | 1 |
| Light cream | ½ cup | 125 mL |

**Super Dressing:** Measure first 7 ingredients into jar. Cover. Shake well. Chill. Makes ¼ cup (60 mL) dressing.

Cook broccoli in water in medium saucepan until tender-crisp. Drain.

Combine mushrooms, pea pods and almonds in large bowl. Add broccoli. Mix. Chill.

Divide lettuce among 8 individual salad plates when ready to serve. Add light cream to dressing in jar. Cover. Shake. Pour over vegetables in bowl. Toss. Spoon over lettuce. Serves 8.

*1 serving: 148 Calories; 10.2 g Total Fat; 214 mg Sodium; 6 g Protein; 11 g Carbohydrate; 5 g Dietary Fiber*

## ARTICHOKE SALAD

*Delicate looking and unusual.*

| | | |
|---|---|---|
| Assorted salad greens | 24 | 24 |
| Radicchio leaves | 8 | 8 |
| Endive leaves | 8 | 8 |
| Alfalfa sprouts | 3 cups | 750 mL |
| Cans of artichoke hearts<br>(14 oz., 398 mL, each),<br>quartered | 2 | 2 |
| Diced green pepper | 2 tbsp. | 30 mL |
| Diced red pepper | 2 tbsp. | 30 mL |
| Diced yellow pepper | 2 tbsp. | 30 mL |
| Large hard-boiled eggs,<br>sliced | 3 | 3 |
| Light Italian dressing<br>(or vinaigrette) | ½ cup | 125 mL |

Divide salad greens among 6 individual salad plates. Add a leaf of radicchio and endive to each plate for interest.

Divide alfalfa sprouts over greens. Spread evenly. Spoon artichoke pieces over sprouts. Sprinkle with diced peppers. Arrange about 2 egg slices alongside of salad.

Drizzle with dressing or serve dressing on the side. Serves 6.

*1 serving: 116 Calories; 4.3 g Total Fat; 580 mg Sodium; 9 g Protein; 14 g Carbohydrate; 6 g Dietary Fiber*

Pictured on page 36.

## MARINATED VEGETABLE SALAD

*To obtain the more authentic zing to this dish, simply omit the water when making the brine. Lots of color in this.*

| | | |
|---|---|---|
| Small onion, sliced into<br>very thin rings | 1 | 1 |
| Cold water, to cover | | |
| Cauliflower florets,<br>cooked tender-crisp | ¾ cup | 175 mL |
| Sliced carrot, cooked<br>tender-crisp | ½ cup | 125 mL |
| Thinly sliced celery | ½ cup | 125 mL |
| Short zucchini fingers | ½ cup | 125 mL |
| Red pepper, cut into<br>matchsticks | ½ cup | 125 mL |
| **BRINE** | | |
| Water | 1 cup | 250 mL |
| White vinegar | 1 cup | 250 mL |
| Can of diced green<br>chilies | 4 oz. | 114 mL |
| Salt | ½ tsp. | 2 mL |
| Pepper | ⅛ tsp. | 0.5 mL |
| Dried whole oregano | ½ tsp. | 2 mL |
| Garlic powder | ½ tsp. | 2 mL |

Put onion rings into cold water. Let stand for 1 hour. Drain.

Combine next 5 ingredients in large bowl. Add onion.

**Brine:** Combine all 7 ingredients in medium saucepan. Bring to a boil. Simmer for 10 minutes. Pour over vegetables. Cool. Mix. Chill for 2 days before serving. Serves 8.

*1 serving: 22 Calories; 0.1 g Total Fat; 281 mg Sodium; 1 g Protein; 6 g Carbohydrate; 1 g Dietary Fiber*

Pictured on front cover.

★★★★★★★★★★★★★★★★★★★★★★★★★★★★

# JAPANESE CABBAGE SALAD

*Out of the ordinary but worth the extra time. Cabbage blends in so well you scarcely know it's there.*

| | | |
|---|---|---|
| Medium head of cabbage, shredded | ½ | ½ |
| Fresh bean sprouts | 2 cups | 500 mL |
| Sliced fresh mushrooms | 2 cups | 500 mL |
| Green onions, chopped | 2 | 2 |
| Sunflower seeds | ¼ cup | 60 mL |
| Toasted sliced or slivered almonds (see Tip, page 21) | ½ cup | 125 mL |
| Toasted sesame seeds (see Tip, page 21) | 2 tbsp. | 30 mL |
| **DRESSING** | | |
| Reserved seasoning packet | 1 | 1 |
| Cooking oil | ½ cup | 125 mL |
| Low-sodium soy sauce | 2 tbsp. | 30 mL |
| White vinegar | 3 tbsp. | 50 mL |
| Granulated sugar | 1 tbsp. | 15 mL |
| Salt | 1 tsp. | 5 mL |
| Pepper | ½ tsp. | 2 mL |
| Package instant noodles, chicken-flavored, broken up, seasoning packet reserved | 3 oz. | 85 g |
| Chow mein noodles | 1½ cups | 375 mL |

Put cabbage and bean sprouts into large bowl. Add mushrooms, green onion and sunflower seeds. Add almonds and sesame seeds. Mix.

**Dressing:** Empty seasoning packet into small bowl. Add next 6 ingredients. Put into container with cover. Shake dressing just before serving. Makes ¾ cup (175 mL) dressing. Pour over cabbage mixture. Toss. Sprinkle dry noodles over top, followed by chow mein noodles. Serves 8.

*1 serving: 327 Calories; 23.2 g Total Fat; 632 mg Sodium; 7 g Protein; 24 g Carbohydrate; 4 g Dietary Fiber*

# TOMATO CHEESE SALAD

*Attractive as well as easy.*

| | | |
|---|---|---|
| Medium tomatoes, seeded and chopped | 8 | 8 |
| Mozzarella cheese, diced | ½ lb. | 225 g |
| Pitted ripe olives | 16-24 | 16-24 |
| Dried sweet basil | ½ tsp. | 2 mL |
| Olive (or cooking) oil | ¼ cup | 60 mL |
| Salt, sprinkle | | |
| Pepper, sprinkle | | |
| Lettuce leaves | 3-4 | 3-4 |

Combine tomato, cheese, olives and basil in large bowl. Stir.

Add olive oil and toss. Sprinkle with salt and pepper. Toss. Add more salt and pepper as needed.

Line large platter with lettuce leaves. Arrange salad on top. Serves 8.

*1 serving: 197 Calories; 16 g Total Fat; 197 mg Sodium; 8 g Protein; 7 g Carbohydrate; 2 g Dietary Fiber*

Pictured on page 71.

# BEAN SALAD

*Pineapple makes this different from the usual bean salad. Dressing has a good bite to it.*

| | | |
|---|---|---|
| Can of kidney beans, drained | 14 oz. | 398 mL |
| Can of pinto (or white) beans, drained | 14 oz. | 398 mL |
| Can of cut green beans, drained | 14 oz. | 398 mL |
| Sliced celery | 1 cup | 250 mL |
| Can of pineapple chunks, drained and juice reserved | 14 oz. | 398 mL |

**DRESSING**

| | | |
|---|---|---|
| Reserved pineapple juice | | |
| Cornstarch | 1 tbsp. | 15 mL |
| Lemon juice | 1 tsp. | 5 mL |
| Red wine vinegar | 1/4 cup | 60 mL |
| Cooking oil | 2 tbsp. | 30 mL |
| Water | 2 tbsp. | 30 mL |
| Dry mustard | 2 tsp. | 10 mL |
| Granulated sugar | 2 tsp. | 10 mL |
| Salt | 1/2 tsp. | 2 mL |
| Dill weed | 1/2 tsp. | 2 mL |
| Pepper | 1/4 tsp. | 1 mL |
| Dried whole oregano | 1/4 tsp. | 1 mL |
| Garlic powder | 1/4 tsp. | 1 mL |
| Onion powder | 1/4 tsp. | 1 mL |

Combine first 5 ingredients in large bowl.

**Dressing:** Stir reserved pineapple juice into cornstarch in small saucepan. Stir in lemon juice.

Add remaining 11 ingredients. Heat, stirring occasionally, until boiling and slightly thickened. Pour over vegetables in bowl. Stir. Cover. Chill for 24 hours, stirring occasionally. Makes 6 cups (1.5 L), enough for 6 servings.

*1 serving:* 208 Calories; 5.4 g Total Fat; 493 mg Sodium; 7 g Protein; 35 g Carbohydrate; 6 g Dietary Fiber

Pictured on page 54.

# BEAN SPROUT SALAD

*This not-so-common salad is excellent.*

| | | |
|---|---|---|
| Frozen pea pods (or 2 cups, 500 mL, fresh) | 6 oz. | 170 g |
| Boiling water, to cover | | |
| Salt | 1 tsp. | 5 mL |
| Fresh bean sprouts | 2 cups | 500 mL |
| Grated cabbage, lightly packed | 1 cup | 250 mL |
| Chopped pimiento | 2 tbsp. | 30 mL |

**DRESSING**

| | | |
|---|---|---|
| Cooking oil | 2 tbsp. | 30 mL |
| Low-sodium soy sauce | 2 tbsp. | 30 mL |
| White vinegar | 2 tbsp. | 30 mL |
| Brown sugar, packed | 2 tbsp. | 30 mL |

Cook pea pods in boiling water and salt in small saucepan for 1 minute. Drain. Cool.

Put bean sprouts, cabbage and pimiento into large bowl. Add pea pods. Mix.

**Dressing:** Mix all 4 ingredients in small bowl. Pour over vegetables in bowl just before serving. Makes 6 tablespoons (100 mL) dressing. Toss. Serves 6.

*1 serving:* 90 Calories; 4.8 g Total Fat; 217 mg Sodium; 3 g Protein; 10 g Carbohydrate; 1 g Dietary Fiber

Pictured on page 53.

# BRUSCHETTA IN A BOWL

*Day-old bread is used to decrease the absorption of the liquid in the salad and for ease of cubing.*

| Cubed day-old Italian bread | 4 cups | 1 L |
| Balsamic vinegar | 1/3 cup | 75 mL |
| Medium cucumber, with peel, quartered lengthwise and sliced | 1 | 1 |
| Medium red or yellow pepper, chopped | 1 | 1 |
| Medium roma (plum) tomatoes, diced | 3 | 3 |
| Freshly ground pepper | 1/4 tsp. | 1 mL |
| Finely chopped fresh sweet basil | 1/4 cup | 60 mL |
| Sliced pitted ripe olives | 1/4 cup | 60 mL |
| Olive oil | 2 tsp. | 10 mL |

Spread bread cubes on large ungreased baking sheet with sides. Bake in 350°F (175°C) oven for 5 minutes. Stir. Bake for 10 to 15 minutes until toasted.

Combine remaining 8 ingredients in large bowl. Add bread cubes. Toss. Makes 7 cups (1.75 L), enough for 7 servings.

*1 serving: 109 Calories; 2.1 g Total Fat; 184 mg Sodium; 3 g Protein; 20 g Carbohydrate; 2 g Dietary Fiber*

# ORIENTAL SALAD

*This is even better the next day.*

**SAKE DRESSING**

| Freshly grated gingerroot | 1/2-1 tsp. | 2-5 mL |
| Sake (rice wine) | 1/4 cup | 60 mL |
| Granulated sugar | 1 tbsp. | 15 mL |
| Low-sodium soy sauce | 2 tbsp. | 30 mL |
| Toasted sesame seeds, optional (see Tip, page 21) | 2 tsp. | 10 mL |
| White wine vinegar | 2 tbsp. | 30 mL |
| Garlic clove, minced | 1 | 1 |
| Dried crushed chilies | 1/4 tsp. | 1 mL |
| Sesame oil | 1 tsp. | 5 mL |
| Broken low-fat instant Chinese noodles | 1 1/4 cups | 300 mL |
| Finely shredded suey choy, lightly packed | 3 cups | 750 mL |
| Julienned jicama | 1 cup | 250 mL |
| Grated carrot | 1/2 cup | 125 mL |
| Green onions, sliced | 4 | 4 |
| Fresh bean sprouts | 2 cups | 500 mL |
| Small red pepper, diced | 1 | 1 |
| Can of water chestnuts, drained, coarsely chopped | 8 oz. | 227 mL |

**Sake Dressing:** Combine first 9 ingredients in jar. Cover. Shake well. Makes 6 tablespoons (100 mL) dressing.

Toss remaining 8 ingredients together in large bowl. Pour dressing over top. Toss. Serves 8.

*1 serving: 95 Calories; 0.9 g Total Fat; 169 mg Sodium; 3 g Protein; 18 g Carbohydrate; 2 g Dietary Fiber*

---

*YOGURT CHEESE: Line strainer with 2 layers of cheesecloth and place over deep bowl. Spoon 4 cups (1 L) plain skim milk yogurt into strainer. Cover loosely with plastic wrap. Drain for 24 hours in refrigerator. Discard whey in bowl several times as yogurt drains. Store yogurt cheese in covered container in refrigerator until expiry date on yogurt container. Makes 2 cups (500 mL).*

# TOMATO RAITA

*Pronounced RI-tah. A cooler to serve with spicy-hot food.*

| Non-fat plain yogurt | 3 cups | 750 mL |
|---|---|---|
| Salt | 1 tsp. | 5 mL |
| Pepper, sprinkle | | |
| Paprika | ½ tsp. | 2 mL |
| Medium tomatoes, cut bite size | 6 | 6 |

Combine yogurt, salt, pepper and paprika in medium bowl. Stir.

Add tomato. Stir to mix. Makes 4 cups (1 L), enough for 4 servings.

*1 serving: 138 Calories; 0.8 g Total Fat; 834 mg Sodium; 11 g Protein; 23 g Carbohydrate; 2 g Dietary Fiber*

Pictured on page 72.

# TOMATO CUKE RAITA

*Pronounced RI-tah. Even though this contains cayenne pepper for flavor it still makes a good cooler.*

| Non-fat plain yogurt | 3 cups | 750 mL |
|---|---|---|
| Ground cumin | ½ tsp. | 2 mL |
| Salt | 1 tsp. | 5 mL |
| Cayenne pepper | ½ tsp. | 2 mL |
| Medium onion, quartered and thinly sliced | 1 | 1 |
| Small cucumber, with peel, halved lengthwise and sliced | 1 | 1 |
| Medium tomato | 1 | 1 |

Combine first 4 ingredients in large bowl. Stir.

Add onion and cucumber.

Dip tomato into boiling water for about 1 minute until it peels easily. Chop. Add to bowl. Stir together. Makes 5 cups (1.25 L), enough for 5 servings.

*1 serving: 101 Calories; 0.4 g Total Fat; 658 mg Sodium; 9 g Protein; 16 g Carbohydrate; 1 g Dietary Fiber*

# SALAD COMBO

*Make this a day ahead. A combination of egg, vegetables and wine vinegar dressing.*

| Salad dressing (or mayonnaise) | ¼ cup | 60 mL |
|---|---|---|
| Red wine vinegar | 1 tbsp. | 15 mL |
| Frozen peas, cooked | 1 cup | 250 mL |
| Chopped celery | ¼ cup | 60 mL |
| Large hard-boiled egg, chopped | 1 | 1 |
| Grated carrot | 2 tbsp. | 30 mL |
| Fresh bean sprouts | 1 cup | 250 mL |
| Onion flakes | 2 tsp. | 10 mL |
| Beef bouillon powder | 1 tsp. | 5 mL |

Measure salad dressing and vinegar into medium bowl. Stir well.

Add remaining 7 ingredients. Toss to coat. Cover. Chill for 24 hours. Toss again before serving. Serves 2.

*1 serving: 281 Calories; 18.4 g Total Fat; 615 mg Sodium; 9 g Protein; 21 g Carbohydrate; 4 g Dietary Fiber*

# BUFFET SALAD

*Lovely contrast of colors and textures. Start this two days in advance for first marinating. Leftover salad can be kept in its marinade in refrigerator for up to one week.*

**MARINADE**

| | | |
|---|---|---|
| Condensed tomato soup | 10 oz. | 284 mL |
| Granulated sugar | ¾ cup | 175 mL |
| White vinegar | ¾ cup | 175 mL |
| Cooking oil | 2 tbsp. | 30 mL |
| Medium red onion, thinly sliced | 1 | 1 |
| Slivered green pepper | ¾ cup | 175 mL |
| Slivered red or yellow pepper | ¾ cup | 175 mL |
| Sliced carrot | 1 cup | 250 mL |
| Boiling water, to cover | | |
| Cauliflower florets | 3½ cups | 875 mL |
| Boiling water, to cover | | |
| Can of sliced water chestnuts, drained | 8 oz. | 227 mL |
| Grated medium Cheddar (or mozzarella) cheese, optional | 1 cup | 250 mL |

**Marinade:** Measure first 7 ingredients into large saucepan. Bring to a boil. Boil for 2 minutes.

Cook carrot in boiling water in medium saucepan until tender-crisp. Drain.

Cook cauliflower in boiling water in same saucepan until tender-crisp. Drain.

Place water chestnuts in 2 quart (2 L) ovenproof container. Add carrot and cauliflower. Pour hot marinade over all. Cool slightly. Cover. Chill for 1 to 2 days before serving. Scoop out with slotted spoon to serve, reserving marinade.

Sprinkle with cheese. Return leftovers to marinade. Cover. Chill. Makes 6½ cups (1.6 L), enough for 13 servings.

*1 serving: 80 Calories; 1.4 g Total Fat; 118 mg Sodium; 2 g Protein; 19 g Carbohydrate; 3 g Dietary Fiber*

# JICAMA AND CORN SALAD

*Jicama (HEE-kah-mah) is often referred to as the Mexican potato. It is sweet and nutty. Great served raw or cooked.*

| | | |
|---|---|---|
| Can of kernel corn, drained | 14 oz. | 398 mL |
| Peeled and diced jicama | 2 cups | 500 mL |
| Diced red pepper | 1 cup | 250 mL |
| Green onions, thinly sliced | 3 | 3 |
| Yogurt Cheese (see Tip, page 63) | ½ cup | 125 mL |
| Freshly squeezed lemon juice | 2 tbsp. | 30 mL |
| Grated lemon peel | 1 tsp. | 5 mL |
| Liquid honey | 1 tbsp. | 15 mL |
| Hot pepper sauce, dash | | |

Combine corn, jicama, red pepper and green onion in large bowl.

Measure remaining 5 ingredients into small bowl. Stir. Fold into corn mixture. Makes 6 cups (1.5 L), enough for 6 servings.

*1 serving: 93 Calories; 0.4 g Total Fat; 179 mg Sodium; 3 g Protein; 22 g Carbohydrate; 4 g Dietary Fiber*

## STUFFED TOMATO SALAD

*A genuine summer salad when you use vine-ripened tomatoes.*

| | | |
|---|---|---|
| Medium tomatoes, hollowed out and inside flesh reserved | 6 | 6 |
| Salt | 1 tsp. | 5 mL |
| Orzo (very small) pasta | ¹⁄₂ cup | 125 mL |
| Boiling water | 4 cups | 1 L |
| Cooking oil (optional) | 1 tsp. | 5 mL |
| Salt | 1 tsp. | 5 mL |
| White (or alcohol-free) wine | ¹⁄₄ cup | 60 mL |
| Balsamic vinegar | 1 tsp. | 5 mL |
| Reserved tomato flesh, chopped (remove some seeds if desired) | 1 cup | 250 mL |
| Basil pesto | 1 tsp. | 5 mL |
| Pectin granules | ¹⁄₂ tsp. | 2 mL |
| Freshly ground pepper, sprinkle | | |
| Green onion, sliced | 1 | 1 |
| Diced green, red, orange or yellow pepper | ¹⁄₄ cup | 60 mL |
| Thinly shredded radicchio | ¹⁄₄ cup | 60 mL |
| Grated carrot | ¹⁄₄ cup | 60 mL |

Sprinkle insides of tomatoes with first amount of salt. Turn upside down on paper towel to drain well.

Cook pasta in boiling water, cooking oil and second amount of salt in large saucepan for 8 to 10 minutes, stirring occasionally, until tender but firm. Drain well. Rinse with cold water. Drain. Turn into medium bowl.

Combine next 6 ingredients in jar or container. Cover. Shake well to mix. Pour over pasta.

Stir in remaining 4 ingredients. Toss well. Stuff each tomato with salad. Makes 6.

*1 stuffed tomato: 119 Calories; 1.3 g Total Fat; 471 mg Sodium; 4 g Protein; 22 g Carbohydrate; 2 g Dietary Fiber*

Pictured on page 54.

## CHEESY PEA SALAD

*A good variation of a green pea salad. Contains egg, cheese and green onion.*

| | | |
|---|---|---|
| Frozen peas, cooked | 1 cup | 250 mL |
| Chopped celery | ¹⁄₂ cup | 125 mL |
| Large hard-boiled egg, chopped | 1 | 1 |
| Diced medium or sharp Cheddar cheese | ¹⁄₄ cup | 60 mL |
| Green onion, thinly sliced | ¹⁄₂ | ¹⁄₂ |
| Chopped pimiento | 1 tsp. | 5 mL |
| **DRESSING** | | |
| Salad dressing (or mayonnaise) | 2 tbsp. | 30 mL |
| Milk | 1¹⁄₂ tsp. | 7 mL |
| Granulated sugar | ¹⁄₄ tsp. | 1 mL |
| Salt, sprinkle | | |
| Pepper, sprinkle | | |

Combine first 6 ingredients in medium bowl.

**Dressing:** Measure all 5 ingredients into small bowl. Stir together well. Makes 3 tablespoons (50 mL) dressing. Pour over salad ingredients. Toss well. Serves 2.

*1 serving: 224 Calories; 15.4 g Total Fat; 305 mg Sodium; 10 g Protein; 13 g Carbohydrate; 4 g Dietary Fiber*

# Bean Soups

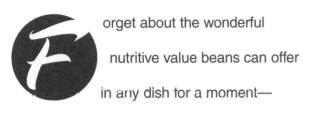

orget about the wonderful

nutritive value beans can offer

in any dish for a moment—

instead, take note of all the different kinds of

beans that make up these great recipes. Bean

soups can be hearty, zesty, nutritious and an

important part of anyone's daily diet. Serve

Fagioli Soup, page 68, as a filling main course

meal, or consider Ham And Bean Soup, page

70, on a frosty winter's day.

## GARBANZO SOUP

*A soft yellow-colored broth with diced potato, ham and garbanzo beans (chick peas). Very hearty.*

| | | |
|---|---|---|
| Lean meaty ham bone (about 2 cups, 500 mL, meat), see Note | 1 | 1 |
| Water | 6 cups | 1.5 L |
| Medium onion, finely chopped | 1 | 1 |
| Garlic clove, minced (or ¼ tsp., 1 mL, powder) | 1 | 1 |
| Bay leaves | 2 | 2 |
| Medium potatoes, diced | 2 | 2 |
| Paprika | ½ tsp. | 2 mL |
| Salt | ¼ tsp. | 1 mL |
| Pepper | ¼ tsp. | 1 mL |
| Can of garbanzo beans (chick peas), with liquid, slightly mashed | 19 oz. | 540 mL |

Combine first 5 ingredients in large pot or Dutch oven. Cover. Boil for about 2 hours. Discard bay leaves. Remove ham bone. Chop ham and return to pot. Discard bone.

Add remaining 5 ingredients. Stir. Cover. Cook until potato is tender. Makes 7½ cups (1.8 L).

*1 cup (250 mL): 228 Calories; 9.3 g Total Fat; 734 mg Sodium; 13 g Protein; 23 g Carbohydrate; 3 g Dietary Fiber*

**Note:** If there is not much meat, add 1 can (6½ oz., 184 g) ham flakes, drained.

## BLACK BEAN SOUP

*Ready in 30 minutes. Excellent the next day.*

| | | |
|---|---|---|
| Lean ground beef | ½ lb. | 225 g |
| Large onion, chopped | 1 | 1 |
| Garlic cloves, minced | 3 | 3 |
| Dried whole oregano | ¼ tsp. | 1 mL |
| Dried thyme | ¼ tsp. | 1 mL |
| Ground cumin | ¼ tsp. | 1 mL |
| Cayenne pepper | ¼ tsp. | 1 mL |
| Salt | ½ tsp. | 2 mL |
| Cans of black beans (19 oz., 540 mL, each), with liquid | 2 | 2 |
| Condensed beef broth (10 oz., 284 mL, each) | 2 | 2 |
| Grated carrot | ½ cup | 125 mL |
| Water | 10 oz. | 284 mL |
| Non-fat sour cream, for garnish | | |
| Finely diced red onion, for garnish | | |

Scramble-fry ground beef, onion and garlic in large pot or Dutch oven until beef is browned and onion is soft. Drain.

Add next 5 ingredients. Sauté for 2 minutes.

Put black beans with liquid and beef broth into blender. Purée until smooth. Add to beef mixture. Add carrot and water. Stir. Simmer for 10 minutes.

Ladle into 8 individual bowls. Garnish with swirl of sour cream and sprinkle of red onion. Makes 8 cups (2 L).

*1 cup (250 mL): 153 Calories; 3.1 g Total Fat; 810 mg Sodium; 13 g Protein; 19 g Carbohydrate; 3 g Dietary Fiber*

## FAGIOLI SOUP

*Faj-OH-lee soup has a good flavor. Lots of beans and pasta. Broth is fairly thin.*

| | | |
|---|---|---|
| Dried navy (white) beans | 1 cup | 250 mL |
| Water | 8 cups | 2 L |
| Ketchup | 1 tbsp. | 15 mL |
| Salt | 1 tbsp. | 15 mL |
| Pepper | ¼ tsp. | 1 mL |
| Garlic powder | ½ tsp. | 2 mL |
| Ground oregano | ¼ tsp. | 1 mL |
| Dried sweet basil | ¼ tsp. | 1 mL |
| Bay leaf | 1 | 1 |
| Uncooked tiny shell pasta | 1 cup | 250 mL |

Combine first 9 ingredients in large saucepan. Bring to a boil. Cover. Simmer for 1½ to 2 hours until beans are tender. Discard bay leaf.

Add pasta. Simmer for about 10 minutes, stirring occasionally, until pasta is tender. Makes about 6½ cups (1.6 L).

*1 cup (250 mL): 168 Calories; 0.7 g Total Fat; 1111 mg Sodium; 9 g Protein; 32 g Carbohydrate; 3 g Dietary Fiber*

*Avoid pasta boiling over by adding 1 tbsp. (15 mL) of cooking oil, butter or hard margarine. It also helps to keep the pasta from sticking.*

## COLOR-FULL BEAN SOUP

*Tasty balance of flavors between the ham and the beans. Name says it all.*

| | | |
|---|---|---|
| Margarine | 1 tbsp. | 15 mL |
| Chopped onion | ½ cup | 125 mL |
| Chopped celery | ½ cup | 125 mL |
| Medium carrot, grated | 1 | 1 |
| Water | 2 cups | 500 mL |
| Medium potato, diced | 1 | 1 |
| Can of mixed beans, with liquid | 19 oz. | 540 mL |
| Bay leaf | 1 | 1 |
| Chili powder | ½ tsp. | 2 mL |
| Parsley flakes | ½ tsp. | 2 mL |
| Pepper | ⅛ tsp. | 0.5 mL |
| Can of ham flakes, drained (or ½ cup, 125 mL, finely chopped cooked ham) | 6½ oz. | 184 g |

Melt margarine in large saucepan. Sauté onion and celery until soft.

Add next 8 ingredients. Bring to a boil. Cover. Simmer for 20 minutes.

Add ham. Stir. Cover. Simmer for 5 minutes. Makes 6 cups (1.5 L).

*1 cup (250 mL):* *201 Calories; 8.4 g Total Fat; 749 mg Sodium; 10 g Protein; 22 g Carbohydrate; 8 g Dietary Fiber*

## BEAN SOUP

*Brownish color with tomato adding a bit of color. Thick soup with a good flavor. Contains canned ham. Simple to make.*

| | | |
|---|---|---|
| Dried navy (white) beans (1 lb., 454 g) | 2⅓ cups | 575 mL |
| Chopped onion | 1¼ cups | 300 mL |
| Garlic clove, minced (or ¼ tsp., 1 mL, powder) | 1 | 1 |
| Can of ham flakes, with liquid (or 1 cup, 250 mL, diced cooked ham) | 6½ oz. | 184 g |
| Can of diced tomatoes, with juice | 14 oz. | 398 mL |
| Water | 6 cups | 1.5 L |
| Salt | 1 tsp. | 5 mL |
| Pepper | ¼ tsp. | 1 mL |

Measure all 8 ingredients into 5 quart (5 L) slow cooker. Stir well. Cover. Cook on Low for 8 to 10 hours or on High for 4 to 5 hours. Taste for salt and pepper, adding more if needed. Makes 9⅔ cups (2.4 L).

*1 cup (250 mL):* *232 Calories; 4.4 g Total Fat; 616 mg Sodium; 15 g Protein; 35 g Carbohydrate; 5 g Dietary Fiber*

*For best results when using canned beans—and for less sodium—drain then rinse the beans in a colander before using them in your recipe.*

## BEAN AND VEGETABLE SOUP

*Use any type of canned beans. Preparation time is 20 minutes.*

| | | |
|---|---|---|
| Margarine | 1 tbsp. | 15 mL |
| Medium onion, diced | 1 | 1 |
| Celery rib, chopped | 1 | 1 |
| Water | 6 cups | 1.5 L |
| Vegetable bouillon powder | 2 tbsp. | 30 mL |
| Coarsely chopped cabbage, lightly packed | 2 cups | 500 mL |
| Diced carrot | 1 cup | 250 mL |
| Can of diced tomatoes, with juice | 14 oz. | 398 mL |
| Can of navy (white) beans, with liquid | 14 oz. | 398 mL |
| Medium potato, diced | 1 | 1 |
| Dried crushed chilies | ¼ tsp. | 1 mL |
| Chopped fresh parsley | 1 tbsp. | 15 mL |
| Freshly ground pepper | ⅛ tsp. | 0.5 mL |

Melt margarine in large pot or Dutch oven. Add onion and celery. Sauté until soft.

Add remaining 10 ingredients. Stir. Cover. Simmer for 40 minutes until vegetables are tender. Makes 11 cups (2.75 L).

*1 cup (250 mL): 90 Calories; 2.3 g Total Fat; 252 mg Sodium; 4 g Protein; 15 g Carbohydrate; 2 g Dietary Fiber*

## HAM AND BEAN SOUP

*A wonderful warm, comforting soup.*

| | | |
|---|---|---|
| Dried navy (white) beans | 2 cups | 500 mL |
| Lean meaty ham bone (or 2 smoked pork hocks) | 1 | 1 |
| Water | 11 cups | 2.75 L |
| Diced carrot | 1 cup | 250 mL |
| Chopped onion | 1¼ cups | 300 mL |
| Chopped celery | ½ cup | 125 mL |
| Salt | 1½ tsp. | 7 mL |
| Pepper | ¼ tsp. | 1 mL |

Combine beans and ham bone in water in large pot or Dutch oven. Cover. Simmer for 1 hour, skimming off foam occasionally, until beans are almost tender. Remove ham bone. Skim off fat. Remove remaining ham from bone. Dice ham and return to pot. Discard bone.

Add remaining 5 ingredients. Stir. Simmer for about 20 minutes until vegetables are tender. Makes 11 cups (2.75 L).

*1 cup (250 mL): 158 Calories; 1.1 g Total Fat; 838 mg Sodium; 12 g Protein; 26 g Carbohydrate; 4 g Dietary Fiber*

**Variation:** Omit ham bone or pork hocks. Add 1 cup (250 mL) chopped cooked ham after beans have been cooked for 1 hour.

1. Mushroom Soup, page 98
2. Mango Tango Salad, page 27
3. Tomato Cheese Salad, page 61

Props Courtesy Of:   Le Gnome, Stokes, The Bay

## LENTIL SOUP

*Spicy hot.*

| | | |
|---|---|---|
| Hot Italian sausages, casings removed, broken up (about ½ lb., 225 g) | 3-4 | 3-4 |
| Hot water | 6 cups | 1.5 L |
| Red lentils | ½ cup | 125 mL |
| Chopped onion | 1 cup | 250 mL |
| Can of tomatoes, with juice | 14 oz. | 398 mL |
| Grated carrot | ½ cup | 125 mL |
| Beef bouillon powder | 2 tsp. | 10 mL |
| Salt | 1 tsp. | 5 mL |

Crumble sausage meat into 3 quart (3 L) microwave-safe dish. Cover loosely with waxed paper. Microwave on high (100%) for about 3 minutes. Stir. Cover. Microwave on high (100%) for about 3 minutes until meat is no longer pink. Drain.

Add remaining 7 ingredients. Stir. Cover. Microwave on high (100%) for 18 to 19 minutes until mixture starts to boil. Cover. Microwave on medium-low (30%) for about 15 minutes until lentils, onion and carrot are cooked. Makes 8⅓ cups (2 L).

*1 cup (250 mL): 105 Calories; 3.6 g Total Fat; 669 mg Sodium; 7 g Protein; 12 g Carbohydrate; 3 g Dietary Fiber*

## EASY BEAN SOUP

*An excellent easy-to-make soup. Vegetables add color.*

| | | |
|---|---|---|
| Cans of brown beans with molasses (14 oz., 398 mL, each) | 2 | 2 |
| Can of ham flakes, with liquid (or 1 cup, 250 mL, diced cooked ham) | 6½ oz. | 184 g |
| Chopped onion | ¾ cup | 175 mL |
| Chopped celery | ½ cup | 125 mL |
| Medium carrots, thinly sliced or diced | 2 | 2 |
| Medium tomatoes, diced | 2 | 2 |
| Garlic powder | ¼ tsp. | 1 mL |
| Chicken bouillon powder | 2 tbsp. | 30 mL |
| Water | 4 cups | 1 L |
| Dried sweet basil | ¼ tsp. | 1 mL |
| Granulated sugar | 1 tsp. | 5 mL |

Combine all 11 ingredients in 3½ quart (3.5 L) slow cooker. Stir. Cover. Cook on Low for 8 to 10 hours or on High for 4 to 5 hours. Makes 9 cups (2.25 L).

*1 cup (250 mL): 165 Calories; 4.8 g Total Fat; 1104 mg Sodium; 9 g Protein; 25 g Carbohydrate; 8 g Dietary Fiber*

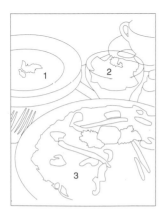

1. Pumpkin Soup, page 94
2. Tomato Raita, page 64
3. Ginger Chicken Salad, page 23

Props Courtesy Of: Club Monaco Everyday, Le Gnome, Stokes, The Bay

# Beef Soups

he distinctive flavors of beef complement almost any kind of soup, which is why you can find it in such a diverse collection of recipes like the ones in this section. If you are a fan of Mexican food, then you must try Spicy Beef And Rice Soup, page 81, and for a more Italian flavor, sample Minestrone, page 75.

## MEATBALL SOUP

*Making this attractive soup is time-consuming but worth it. The tiny meatballs look nice in the soup.*

| | | |
|---|---|---|
| Can of diced tomatoes, with juice | 14 oz. | 398 mL |
| Chopped celery | ½ cup | 125 mL |
| Chopped onion | 1¼ cups | 300 mL |
| Medium potato, diced | 1 | 1 |
| Beef bouillon powder | 2 tbsp. | 30 mL |
| Water | 6 cups | 1.5 L |
| Garlic powder | ¼ tsp. | 1 mL |
| Parsley flakes | 1 tsp. | 5 mL |
| Salt | ½ tsp. | 2 mL |
| Granulated sugar | ½ tsp. | 2 mL |
| Dried sweet basil | ½ tsp. | 2 mL |
| Pepper | ⅛ tsp. | 0.5 mL |
| **MEATBALLS** | | |
| Dry bread crumbs | ¼ cup | 60 mL |
| Salt | ¼ tsp. | 1 mL |
| Pepper | ⅛ tsp. | 0.5 mL |
| Seasoned salt | ¼ tsp. | 1 mL |
| Lean ground beef | ½ lb. | 225 g |

Combine first 12 ingredients in large pot or Dutch oven. Stir. Bring to a boil. Simmer, uncovered, for 30 minutes.

**Meatballs:** Mix bread crumbs, salt, pepper and seasoned salt in medium bowl. Add ground beef. Mix well. Shape into ½ inch (12 mm) balls. Arrange on greased baking sheet with sides. Bake in 375°F (190°C) oven for 5 to 7 minutes. Add to tomato mixture. Simmer for 15 minutes. Makes 10½ cups (2.6 L).

*1 cup (250 mL): 88 Calories; 3.7 g Total Fat; 671 mg Sodium; 6 g Protein; 9 g Carbohydrate; 1 g Dietary Fiber*

Pictured on page 108.

## MINESTRONE

*A good substantial soup. Easy to make for a rainy day meal—or any day.*

| | | |
|---|---|---|
| Cooking oil | 1 tbsp. | 15 mL |
| Lean ground beef | 1 lb. | 454 g |
| Chopped onion | 1½ cups | 375 mL |
| Chopped celery | 1½ cups | 375 mL |
| Grated carrot | ¾ cup | 175 mL |
| Can of kidney beans, with liquid | 14 oz. | 398 mL |
| Can of diced tomatoes, with juice | 14 oz. | 398 mL |
| Water | 4 cups | 1 L |
| Beef bouillon powder | 4 tsp. | 20 mL |
| Salt | 1 tsp. | 5 mL |
| Pepper | ¼ tsp. | 1 mL |
| Garlic powder | ¼ tsp. | 1 mL |
| Dried whole oregano | ½ tsp. | 2 mL |
| Dried sweet basil | ½ tsp. | 2 mL |
| Coarsely grated cabbage, lightly packed | 3 cups | 750 mL |
| Uncooked tiny shell pasta | ¾ cup | 175 mL |
| Grated Parmesan cheese, sprinkle | | |

Heat cooking oil in large frying pan. Add ground beef, onion, celery and carrot. Scramble-fry until beef is no longer pink. Drain. Turn into large pot or Dutch oven.

Add next 9 ingredients. Stir. Heat until boiling.

Add cabbage and pasta. Stir. Simmer, uncovered, for 20 minutes, stirring occasionally.

Sprinkle individual servings with cheese. Makes 12 cups (3 L).

*1 cup (250 mL): 137 Calories; 4.2 g Total Fat; 559 mg Sodium; 11 g Protein; 15 g Carbohydrate; 3 g Dietary Fiber*

## BEEFY VEGETABLE SOUP

*Beef and vegetables are in a dark, flavorful broth.*

| | | |
|---|---|---|
| Boneless beef (such as stew beef), diced | ¼ lb. | 113 g |
| Water | 3 cups | 750 mL |
| Chopped onion | ½ cup | 125 mL |
| Medium carrot, diced | 1 | 1 |
| Diced rutabaga (yellow turnip) | ⅓ cup | 75 mL |
| Small bay leaf | 1 | 1 |
| Parsley flakes | ¹⁄₁₆ tsp. | 0.5 mL |
| Ground rosemary (or sage) | ¹⁄₁₆ tsp. | 0.5 mL |
| Beef bouillon powder | 1 tbsp. | 15 mL |
| Pepper | ¹⁄₁₆ tsp. | 0.5 mL |

Place beef in medium saucepan. Add water. Cover. Cook for 1 hour.

Add remaining 8 ingredients. Stir. Cover. Boil gently for about 30 minutes until vegetables are tender. Discard bay leaf. Makes about 4 cups (1 L).

*1 cup (250 mL): 54 Calories; 1.2 g Total Fat; 544 mg Sodium; 5 g Protein; 5 g Carbohydrate; 1 g Dietary Fiber*

*A quick and easy way to shape 1 inch (2.5 cm) meatballs is to pat the meatball mixture into a 1 inch (2.5 cm) thick square on waxed paper; then cut the square into 1 inch (2.5 cm) cubes. Dip your hands in water and gently roll the cubes into balls.*

## ONION SOUP

*This always hits the spot! Nice beefy broth.*

| | | |
|---|---|---|
| Thin sirloin steak, diced | 1 lb. | 454 g |
| Water | 9 cups | 2.25 L |
| Chopped celery | 1 cup | 250 mL |
| Thinly sliced carrot | 2 cups | 500 mL |
| Diced potato | 2 cups | 500 mL |
| Bay leaf | 1 | 1 |
| Garlic cloves | 2 | 2 |
| Salt | 2 tsp. | 10 mL |
| Pepper | ½ tsp. | 2 mL |
| Beef bouillon powder | 3 tbsp. | 50 mL |
| Sliced onion | 4 cups | 1 L |
| French bread slices, toasted | 10 | 10 |
| Grated part-skim mozzarella cheese | 1 cup | 250 mL |

Combine steak and water in large saucepan. Bring to a boil. Boil slowly for 15 minutes.

Add next 9 ingredients. Return to a boil. Simmer for about 1 hour until vegetables are tender. Discard bay leaf.

Ladle into individual ovenproof soup bowls. Lay slice of toast on top of each serving, cutting to fit if necessary. Sprinkle each with cheese. Bake in 450°F (230°C) oven until cheese is melted and browned. If bowls aren't ovenproof, place toast slices on ungreased baking sheet to melt and brown cheese. Transfer to bowls. Makes 10 cups (2.5 L).

*1 cup (250 mL):* 186 Calories; 4.6 g Total Fat; 1274 mg Sodium; 16 g Protein; 20 g Carbohydrate; 2 g Dietary Fiber

## BEEF STOCK

*The slow cooker is ideal for getting all the flavor from soup bones. Requires no minding.*

| | | |
|---|---|---|
| Meaty beef soup bone (see Note) | 3 lbs. | 1.4 kg |
| Medium carrots, chopped | 2 | 2 |
| Medium onion, chopped | 1 | 1 |
| Celery ribs, chopped | 2 | 2 |
| Parsley flakes (or ⅓ cup, 75 mL, fresh) | 4 tsp. | 20 mL |
| Salt | 1 tsp. | 5 mL |
| Bay leaf | 1 | 1 |
| Whole peppercorns | 6 | 6 |
| Ground thyme | ⅛ tsp. | 0.5 mL |
| Water | 7 cups | 1.75 L |

Roast bone, uncovered, in small roaster in 350°F (175°C) oven for about 1 hour until browned. Transfer to 5 quart (5 L) slow cooker.

Add remaining 9 ingredients. Stir. Cover. Cook on Low for 10 to 12 hours or on High for 5 to 6 hours. Remove bone. Cut off beef. Chop and reserve for future use. Discard bone. Strain stock into container. Chill. Spoon off fat from top. Discard vegetables. Use in any beef soup recipe. Makes 5¼ cups (1.3 L).

*1 cup (250 mL):* 7 Calories; trace Total Fat; 524 mg Sodium; trace Protein; 2 g Carbohydrate; trace Dietary Fiber

**Note:** For a more flavorful stock, have your butcher saw beef bone into pieces.

# BEEF BARLEY SOUP

*A meaty soup. Make a double batch and freeze whatever is left.*

| | | |
|---|---|---|
| Cooking oil | 1 tbsp. | 15 mL |
| Round steak (or stew beef), diced | 1/2 lb. | 225 g |
| Pearl barley | 3 tbsp. | 50 mL |
| Beef bouillon cube (1/5 oz., 6 g) | 1 | 1 |
| Bay leaf | 1/2 | 1/2 |
| Salt | 1/2 tsp. | 2 mL |
| Pepper | 1/0 tsp. | 0.5 mL |
| Water | 5 cups | 1.25 L |
| Diced onion | 1/2 cup | 125 mL |
| Thinly sliced or diced carrot | 1/2 cup | 125 mL |
| Parsley flakes | 1/2 tsp. | 2 mL |
| Diced potato | 1/2 cup | 125 mL |

Heat cooking oil in large saucepan. Add steak. Brown well.

Add next 6 ingredients. Cover. Simmer for 2 hours.

Add onion, carrot and parsley flakes. Simmer for 20 minutes.

Add potato. Stir. Simmer until tender. Discard bay leaf. Check for salt and pepper, adding more if needed. Makes 5 1/3 cups (1.3 L).

*1 cup (250 mL): 129 Calories; 3.8 g Total Fat; 478 mg Sodium; 12 g Protein; 11 g Carbohydrate; 2 g Dietary Fiber*

# HAMBURGER SOUP

*Double the ingredients and make this for your family. Wholesome and hearty!*

| | | |
|---|---|---|
| Lean ground beef | 1/2 lb. | 225 g |
| Finely chopped onion | 1/4 cup | 60 mL |
| Finely chopped celery | 1/4 cup | 60 mL |
| Medium carrot, cut in half lengthwise, then thinly sliced | 1 | 1 |
| Medium potato, diced | 1 | 1 |
| Water | 3 cups | 750 mL |
| Beef bouillon powder | 1 tbsp. | 15 mL |
| Condensed tomato soup | 10 oz. | 284 mL |

Scramble-fry ground beef in medium saucepan until no longer pink. Drain.

Stir in onion and celery. Scramble-fry for 3 minutes.

Stir in carrot, potato, water and bouillon powder. Bring to a boil. Reduce heat. Cover. Simmer for 20 minutes.

Stir in soup. Heat through. Makes 5 cups (1.25 L).

*1 cup (250 mL): 143 Calories; 4.9 g Total Fat; 805 mg Sodium; 10 g Protein; 15 g Carbohydrate; 2 g Dietary Fiber*

*If you have leftover bits of cheese, grate them and bag all together. Freeze and use as garnish on top of soups.*

## Bok Choy Beef Soup

*Make the rest of the soup while the beef is marinating.*

| Flank steak | ½ lb. | 225 g |
|---|---|---|
| Cornstarch | 1 tsp. | 5 mL |
| Grated gingerroot | ½ tsp. | 2 mL |
| Cooking (or sesame) oil | ½ tsp. | 2 mL |
| Soy sauce | 1 tbsp. | 15 mL |
| Dried crushed chilies, just a pinch | | |
| Condensed beef broth (10 oz., 284 mL, each) | 3 | 3 |
| Water | 3 cups | 750 mL |
| Julienned carrot | 1 cup | 250 mL |
| Finely slivered onion | ½ cup | 125 mL |
| Large ribs of bok choy, cut into ½ x 2 inch (12 mm x 5 cm) pieces | 6 | 6 |
| Thinly sliced green onion, for garnish | | |
| Toasted sesame seeds, for garnish (see Tip, page 21) | | |

Slice steak with grain into 2 inch (5 cm) strips. Cut strips against grain into ⅛ inch (3 mm) slivers. Beef should be very finely cut.

Combine cornstarch, ginger, cooking oil, soy sauce and crushed chilies in small bowl. Add beef slivers. Stir to combine. Cover. Chill for 30 minutes.

Pour broth and water into large saucepan. Bring to a boil. Add carrot and onion. Cover. Simmer for 15 minutes. Stir in marinated beef and bok choy. Boil, uncovered, for 3 minutes.

Garnish each serving with green onion and sesame seeds. Makes 8 cups (2 L).

*1 cup (250 mL): 95 Calories; 2.4 g Total Fat; 763 mg Sodium; 12 g Protein; 6 g Carbohydrate; 1 g Dietary Fiber*

## Beef Barley Soup

*A hearty soup made with a tomato base.*

| Beef stew meat, diced small | 1 lb. | 454 g |
|---|---|---|
| Sliced or chopped carrot | 1¼ cups | 300 mL |
| Chopped onion | 1¼ cups | 300 mL |
| Chopped celery | ¾ cup | 175 mL |
| Water | 5 cups | 1.25 L |
| Parsley flakes | 1 tsp. | 5 mL |
| Pepper | ¼ tsp. | 1 mL |
| Granulated sugar | 1 tsp. | 5 mL |
| Beef bouillon powder | 2 tbsp. | 30 mL |
| Pearl barley | ½ cup | 125 mL |
| Tomato sauce (7½ oz., 213 mL, each) | 2 | 2 |

Place all 11 ingredients in 5 quart (5 L) slow cooker. Stir. Cover. Cook on Low for 8 to 10 hours or on High for 4 to 5 hours. Makes 10¼ cups (2.5 L).

*1 cup (250 mL): 113 Calories; 1.8 g Total Fat; 637 mg Sodium; 9 g Protein; 16 g Carbohydrate; 3 g Dietary Fiber*

*If bok choy is not available, use an equal amount of spinach or cabbage.*

# BEEF AND SPLIT PEA SOUP

*Makes a large batch. Make half the recipe for a small slow cooker. Chunky, colorful and thick. Freezes well.*

| | | |
|---|---|---|
| Lean ground beef | 1 lb. | 454 g |
| Chopped onion | 1 cup | 250 mL |
| Dried yellow split peas | 1/2 cup | 125 mL |
| Pearl barley | 1/2 cup | 125 mL |
| Uncooked long grain converted rice | 1/2 cup | 125 mL |
| Parsley flakes | 1 tsp. | 5 mL |
| Liquid gravy browner | 1/2 tsp. | 2 mL |
| Cans of diced tomatoes (14 oz., 398 mL, each), with juice | 2 | 2 |
| Condensed tomato soup | 10 oz. | 284 mL |
| Beef bouillon powder | 1 tbsp. | 15 mL |
| Salt | 2 tsp. | 10 mL |
| Pepper | 1/2 tsp. | 2 mL |
| Water | 12 cups | 3 L |
| Ground thyme | 1/4 tsp. | 1 mL |
| Uncooked tiny shell pasta | 2 cups | 500 mL |

Scramble-fry ground beef in small non-stick frying pan until no longer pink. Drain well.

Combine next 13 ingredients in 5 quart (5 L) slow cooker. Add ground beef. Stir. Cover. Cook on Low for 9 to 11 hours or on High for 4 1/2 to 5 1/2 hours.

Add pasta. Stir. Cover. Cook on High for 15 to 20 minutes until pasta is tender. Makes 17 1/3 cups (4.3 L).

*1 cup (250 mL): 177 Calories; 3 g Total Fat; 631 mg Sodium; 10 g Protein; 28 g Carbohydrate; 3 g Dietary Fiber*

# BEEF AND BARLEY SOUP

*A meaty and satisfying soup.*

| | | |
|---|---|---|
| Stew meat, trimmed of fat, diced into 1/4 inch (6 mm) pieces | 3/4 lb. | 340 g |
| Pearl barley | 1/3 cup | 75 mL |
| Can of diced tomatoes, with juice | 14 oz. | 398 mL |
| Liquid gravy browner | 1 tsp. | 5 mL |
| Water | 7 cups | 1.75 L |
| Finely shredded cabbage, lightly packed | 1 cup | 250 mL |
| Thinly sliced carrot | 1/2 cup | 125 mL |
| Thinly sliced celery | 1/2 cup | 125 mL |
| Chopped onion | 1 cup | 250 mL |
| Diced rutabaga (yellow turnip) | 1/2 cup | 125 mL |
| Beef bouillon powder | 1 tbsp. | 15 mL |
| Salt | 1/2 tsp. | 2 mL |
| Pepper | 1/4 tsp. | 1 mL |
| Parsley flakes | 1/2 tsp. | 2 mL |
| Dried sweet basil | 1/2 tsp. | 2 mL |

Combine beef, barley, tomatoes with juice, gravy browner and water in large pot or Dutch oven. Stir. Simmer, uncovered, for 1 hour. Skim off foam as necessary.

Add remaining 10 ingredients. Stir. Simmer, uncovered, for about 40 minutes, stirring occasionally. Makes 6 1/2 cups (1.6 L).

*1 cup (250 mL): 127 Calories; 2.2 g Total Fat; 650 mg Sodium; 11 g Protein; 17 g Carbohydrate; 4 g Dietary Fiber*

## TWO-DAY BARLEY SOUP

*Prepare the beef on Day One. Cook the soup on Day Two.*

| | | |
|---|---|---|
| Beef shanks, bone in | 3 | 3 |
| Water | 10 cups | 2.5 L |
| Beef bouillon powder | 2 tbsp. | 30 mL |
| Celery ribs, with leaves | 4-5 | 4-5 |
| Small onion | 1 | 1 |
| Bay leaves | 2 | 2 |
| Whole peppercorns | 10 | 10 |
| Salt | 1 tsp. | 5 mL |
| Freshly ground pepper, to taste | | |
| Pearl barley | ⅔ cup | 150 mL |
| Medium carrots, quartered lengthwise and sliced | 3 | 3 |
| Chopped onion | 1 cup | 250 mL |
| Chopped celery | 1 cup | 250 mL |
| Medium potatoes, diced | 2-3 | 2-3 |
| Condensed tomato soup | 10 oz. | 284 mL |

**Day 1:** Combine first 9 ingredients in large pot or Dutch oven. Bring to a boil. Skim off any foam. Cover. Simmer for 2 hours until beef is very tender. Remove shanks. Dice beef. Discard bones. Cover. Strain broth into large bowl. Cover. Chill beef and broth until next day.

**Day 2:** Remove hardened fat from surface of beef broth. Discard. Heat broth in stockpot until boiling. Add barley, carrot, onion and celery. Cover. Simmer for 45 minutes until barley is almost cooked. Add potato. Cover. Simmer for about 15 minutes. Stir in soup and diced beef. Heat through. Makes 12 cups (3 L).

*1 cup (250 mL): 147 Calories; 2.5 g Total Fat; 746 mg Sodium; 12 g Protein; 20 g Carbohydrate; 3 g Dietary Fiber*

*Fat on the top of soup can be removed easily by dropping 3 or 4 ice cubes into the pot. The fat will stick to the ice cubes and the cubes can then be scooped out.*

## SPICY BEEF AND RICE SOUP

*Eliminate the crushed chilies for a milder flavor.*

| | | |
|---|---|---|
| Minute steak | 1 lb. | 454 g |
| Cooking oil | 2 tsp. | 10 mL |
| Garlic clove, minced | 1 | 1 |
| Finely chopped onion | ¼ cup | 60 mL |
| Chopped fresh sweet basil | 2 tbsp. | 30 mL |
| Dried whole oregano | ½ tsp. | 2 mL |
| Dried thyme | ¼ tsp. | 1 mL |
| Dried crushed chilies | ¼ tsp. | 1 mL |
| Salt | ½ tsp. | 2 mL |
| Pepper | ⅛ tsp. | 0.5 mL |
| Water | 5 cups | 1.25 L |
| Can of diced Mexican-style tomatoes, drained | 14 oz. | 398 mL |
| Uncooked long grain white rice | ½ cup | 125 mL |
| Chili powder | ¼ tsp. | 1 mL |
| Hot pepper sauce, to taste | | |
| Chopped fresh cilantro (coriander) | 2 tbsp. | 30 mL |

Cut steak into 1 inch (2.5 cm) strips, then across into 1 inch (2.5 cm) cubes. Heat cooking oil in non-stick frying pan. Add steak, garlic and onion. Stir-fry just until beef is no longer pink.

Remove to medium bowl. Add basil, oregano, thyme, crushed chilies, salt and pepper. Cover. Let stand in refrigerator for 30 minutes.

Combine water, tomatoes, rice, chili powder and hot pepper sauce in large pot or Dutch oven. Bring to a boil. Reduce heat. Cover tightly. Simmer for 20 minutes. Add beef mixture. Stir to heat thoroughly.

Gently stir in cilantro. Serve immediately. Makes 8 cups (2 L).

*1 cup (250 mL): 157 Calories; 5.4 g Total Fat; 402 mg Sodium; 14 g Protein; 12 g Carbohydrate; trace Dietary Fiber*

## MEATY SOUP

*A meal-type savory soup. Serve with biscuits and a dessert.*

| | | |
|---|---|---|
| Stew beef, trimmed of fat, cut into ½ inch (12 mm) cubes | 1 lb. | 454 g |
| Water | 7 cups | 1.75 L |
| Liquid gravy browner | 1 tsp. | 5 mL |
| Chopped onion | 1½ cups | 375 mL |
| Grated potato | 1½ cups | 375 mL |
| Grated carrot | ¾ cup | 175 mL |
| Paprika | 2 tsp. | 10 mL |
| Parsley flakes | 2 tsp. | 10 mL |
| Ketchup | 1 tbsp. | 15 mL |
| Ground thyme | ⅛ tsp. | 0.5 mL |
| Salt | 1½ tsp. | 7 mL |
| Pepper | ¼ tsp. | 1 mL |

Heat beef, water and gravy browner in large pot or Dutch oven. Cover. Boil gently for 1½ hours. Beef should be very tender.

Add remaining 9 ingredients. Stir. Cover. Boil gently, stirring occasionally, for 25 to 35 minutes until vegetables are tender. Makes 8 cups (2 L).

*1 cup (250 mL): 99 Calories; 1.9 g Total Fat; 580 mg Sodium; 10 g Protein; 10 g Carbohydrate; 1 g Dietary Fiber*

# Chicken Soups

**D**on't wait for the cold and flu season to descend upon your household—serve any one of these marvelous chicken soup recipes year-round. One feature of chicken soup is its economical use of chicken—from breast to bone, every part can be used to make a flavorful dish.

## CHICKEN VEGETABLE SOUP

*A colorful soup. Lots of chicken.*

| | | |
|---|---|---|
| Boneless, skinless chicken breast halves, diced (about 3) | ¾ lb. | 340 g |
| Chopped onion | 1 cup | 250 mL |
| Thinly sliced carrot | 1⅓ cups | 325 mL |
| Diced celery | ½ cup | 125 mL |
| Diced rutabaga (yellow turnip) | ½ cup | 125 mL |
| Diced potato | 2 cups | 500 mL |
| Chicken bouillon powder | 1 tbsp. | 15 mL |
| Salt | 1 tsp. | 5 mL |
| Pepper | ¼ tsp. | 1 mL |
| Ground thyme | ¼ tsp. | 1 mL |
| Water | 4 cups | 1 L |

**Liquid gravy browner, to color slightly (optional)**

Place first 11 ingredients in 5 quart (5 L) slow cooker. Stir. Cover. Cook on Low for 8 to 10 hours or on High for 4 to 5 hours. If vegetables are large and not quite tender, turn heat to High for a few minutes.

Add gravy browner just before serving. Taste for salt and pepper, adding more if needed. Makes 8 cups (2 L).

*1 cup (250 mL): 105 Calories; 0.9 g Total Fat; 635 mg Sodium; 12 g Protein; 12 g Carbohydrate; 2 g Dietary Fiber*

# MULLIGATAWNY

*This has a mild curry flavor. If you're into the real thing you will want to double the curry powder.*

| | | |
|---|---|---|
| Boneless, skinless chicken breast halves (about 2) | ½ lb. | 225 g |
| Dried yellow split peas | ⅓ cup | 75 mL |
| Boiling water | 8 cups | 2 L |
| Margarine | 2 tbsp. | 30 mL |
| Chopped onion | 1½ cups | 375 mL |
| Large cooking apple (such as McIntosh), peeled, cored and diced | 1 | 1 |
| Curry powder | 1 tbsp. | 15 mL |
| All-purpose flour | ¼ cup | 60 mL |
| Salt | ½ tsp. | 2 mL |
| Pepper | ⅛ tsp. | 0.5 mL |
| Diced carrot | ⅔ cup | 150 mL |
| Diced celery | ⅔ cup | 150 mL |
| Ground mace | ⅛ tsp. | 0.5 mL |
| Ground cloves | ⅛ tsp. | 0.5 mL |
| Can of diced tomatoes, with juice | 14 oz. | 398 mL |
| Skim evaporated milk | 1 cup | 250 mL |
| Cooked long grain white rice (optional) | 2¼ cups | 560 mL |

Combine chicken and split peas in boiling water in large pot or Dutch oven. Cover. Boil gently for about 10 minutes until chicken is tender. Skim off foam. Remove chicken to plate. Dice. Return to pot.

Melt margarine in large frying pan. Add onion, apple and curry powder. Sauté for about 5 minutes until onion is soft.

Mix in flour, salt and pepper. Stir into chicken mixture.

Add carrot, celery, mace, cloves and tomatoes with juice. Stir. Simmer, uncovered, for 30 to 40 minutes until carrot is tender.

Stir in evaporated milk. Heat through.

Scoop ¼ cup (60 mL) rice into each soup bowl. Fill with soup. Makes 9 cups (2.25 L).

*1 cup (250 mL): 151 Calories; 3.5 g Total Fat; 319 mg Sodium; 12 g Protein; 19 g Carbohydrate; 3 g Dietary Fiber*

*To quickly mince an onion, peel and quarter it. Place the sections in a blender and cover with cold water. Turn the blender on high for about 3 seconds, then turn it off. Repeat until onion is blended. Pour the mixture into a sieve and let the water drain out.*

## CHICKEN AND CORN SOUP

*Popular with early settlers. Different and delicious.*

| | | |
|---|---|---|
| Chicken Stock (see page 86) | 8 cups | 2 L |
| Chopped celery | ⅔ cup | 150 mL |
| Kernel corn (fresh or frozen) | 2 cups | 500 mL |
| Linguine pasta, broken into 1 inch (2.5 cm) pieces before measuring | 1 cup | 250 mL |
| Diced cooked chicken | 2 cups | 500 mL |
| Parsley flakes | ½ tsp. | 2 mL |
| Turmeric | ¼ tsp. | 1 mL |
| Salt | ¼ tsp. | 1 mL |
| Pepper | ⅛ tsp. | 0.5 mL |
| Large hard-boiled eggs, chopped | 2 | 2 |
| Light frozen whipped topping, thawed (for garnish) | 2 cups | 500 mL |
| Chopped green onion, for garnish | | |

Measure first 10 ingredients into large pot or Dutch oven. Stir. Bring to a boil. Cover. Cook for about 15 minutes until vegetables are tender.

Garnish individual servings with dab of whipped topping and green onion. Makes about 9 cups (2.25 L).

*1 cup (250 mL): 148 Calories; 3.2 g Total Fat; 747 mg Sodium; 14 g Protein; 16 g Carbohydrate; 1 g Dietary Fiber*

## CHICKEN AND HAM SOUP

*Quite a mixture in this tasty soup. Enjoyed by all.*

| | | |
|---|---|---|
| Long grain white rice | ½ cup | 125 mL |
| Water | 4 cups | 1 L |
| Uncooked elbow macaroni | ¾ cup | 175 mL |
| Chopped onion | 1 cup | 250 mL |
| Grated carrot | ½ cup | 125 mL |
| Condensed cream of chicken soup | 10 oz. | 284 mL |
| Can of ham flakes, with liquid | 6½ oz. | 184 g |
| Can of chicken flakes, with liquid | 6½ oz. | 184 g |
| Skim evaporated milk | ⅔ cup | 150 mL |
| Chicken bouillon powder | 1 tsp. | 5 mL |
| Salt | 1 tsp. | 5 mL |
| Can of diced tomatoes, with juice | 14 oz. | 398 mL |

Measure rice and water into large saucepan. Cover. Cook for 10 minutes.

Add macaroni, onion and carrot. Stir. Cook for 5 to 7 minutes until macaroni is tender.

Add next 6 ingredients. Stir. Heat until simmering.

Add tomatoes with juice. Stir. Heat until almost boiling. Add a bit more water if too thick. Makes 9 cups (2.25 L).

*1 cup (250 mL): 243 Calories; 8 g Total Fat; 1096 mg Sodium; 12 g Protein; 30 g Carbohydrate; 2 g Dietary Fiber*

# CHICKEN CURRY SOUP

*Similar to a chowder. An easy from-the-shelf soup. More curry powder may be added as desired.*

| | | |
|---|---|---|
| Condensed cream of chicken soup | 10 oz. | 284 mL |
| Soup can of milk | 10 oz. | 284 mL |
| Can of chicken flakes, with liquid, broken up | 6¹/₂ oz. | 184 g |
| Grated carrot | ¹/₂ cup | 125 mL |
| Minced onion (or 1 tsp., 5 mL, flakes) | 1 tbsp. | 15 mL |
| Instant rice | ¹/₂ cup | 125 mL |
| Curry powder, large measure | ¹/₂ tsp. | 2 mL |
| Chicken bouillon powder | 2¹/₂ tsp. | 12 mL |
| Water | 2 cups | 500 mL |

Place all 9 ingredients in large saucepan. Bring to a boil, stirring often. Boil gently for 10 to 15 minutes until carrot is cooked. Add a bit more water if too thick. Makes 4 cups (1 L).

*1 cup (250 mL): 238 Calories; 9.3 g Total Fat; 1273 mg Sodium; 16 g Protein; 22 g Carbohydrate; 1 g Dietary Fiber*

# ORIENTAL CHICKEN SOUP

*Clear broth with fine egg threads and vegetables.*

| | | |
|---|---|---|
| Condensed chicken broth (10 oz., 284 mL, each) | 2 | 2 |
| Water | 2¹/₂ cups | 625 mL |
| Sliced fresh mushrooms | ¹/₂ cup | 125 mL |
| Thinly sliced bok choy | 1 cup | 250 mL |
| Finely chopped celery | ¹/₃ cup | 75 mL |
| Diced cooked chicken | ¹/₂ cup | 125 mL |
| Chopped water chestnuts | 2 tbsp. | 30 mL |
| Salt | ¹/₂ tsp. | 2 mL |
| Pepper | ¹/₈ tsp. | 0.5 mL |
| Large egg, fork-beaten | 1 | 1 |

Combine first 9 ingredients in large saucepan. Bring to a boil. Simmer for 15 minutes.

Add egg to boiling liquid slowly in thin stream as you whisk with fork. It will cook in fine threads. Makes a generous 5 cups (1.25 L).

*1 cup (250 mL): 86 Calories; 2.9 g Total Fat; 1067 mg Sodium; 12 g Protein; 3 g Carbohydrate; trace Dietary Fiber*

*If your soup is too salty, grate a raw potato and add it to the soup. The potato absorbs the salt.*

## CHICKEN STOCK

*Easy to make soup from scratch, beginning with stock. No need to keep an eye on this.*

| | | |
|---|---|---|
| Chicken drumsticks (or meaty backs and necks) | 1 lb. | 454 g |
| Medium onion, chopped | 1 | 1 |
| Medium carrot, chopped | 1 | 1 |
| Chopped celery | 1 cup | 250 mL |
| Small bay leaf | 1 | 1 |
| Parsley flakes | 1 tsp. | 5 mL |
| Whole cloves | 4 | 4 |
| Salt | 2 tsp. | 10 mL |
| Pepper | $\frac{1}{2}$ tsp. | 2 mL |
| Ground thyme | $\frac{1}{4}$ tsp. | 1 mL |
| Liquid gravy browner (optional) | $\frac{1}{2}$ tsp. | 2 mL |
| Water, to cover | | |

Place chicken in $3\frac{1}{2}$ quart (3.5 L) slow cooker. Add next 10 ingredients.

Pour water over all. Stir. Cover. Cook on Low for 8 to 10 hours or on High for 4 to 5 hours. Skim off foam if needed. Remove chicken and discard skin. Chop chicken and reserve for soup. Strain broth. Chill. Spoon off fat from top. Makes $4\frac{1}{3}$ cups (1 L).

*1 cup (250 mL): 9 Calories; 0.2 g Total Fat; 1367 mg Sodium; trace Protein; 2 g Carbohydrate; trace Dietary Fiber*

## EASY CHICKEN STOCK

Chicken stock can be made by combining 8 cups (2 L) boiling water and 3 tbsp. (50 mL) chicken bouillon powder.

## CHICKEN SOUP

*Good flavor with vegetables and a hint of pepper.*

| | | |
|---|---|---|
| Chicken Stock (see page 86) | 8 cups | 2 L |
| Can of stewed tomatoes, with juice, broken up | 14 oz. | 398 mL |
| Chopped onion | 1 cup | 250 mL |
| Medium carrots, diced or thinly sliced | 2 | 2 |
| Grated potato, packed | 1 cup | 250 mL |
| Salt | $\frac{1}{2}$ tsp. | 2 mL |
| Pepper | $\frac{1}{2}$ tsp. | 2 mL |
| Diced cooked chicken | 2 cups | 500 mL |

Put first 7 ingredients into large stockpot or Dutch oven. Bring to a boil, stirring occasionally. Cover. Simmer gently for about 1 hour.

Add chicken. Stir. Simmer for 5 minutes. Makes $6\frac{2}{3}$ cups (1.65 L).

*1 cup (250 mL): 143 Calories; 2.5 g Total Fat; 1292 mg Sodium; 16 g Protein; 14 g Carbohydrate; 2 g Dietary Fiber*

*Soups & Salads*

## CHICKEN NOODLE SOUP

*Good soup anytime—whether you're healthy or sick.*

| Chicken Stock (see page 86) | 8 cups | 2 L |
|---|---|---|
| Diced carrot | ½ cup | 125 mL |
| Diced celery | ½ cup | 125 mL |
| Chopped onion | ½ cup | 125 mL |
| Bacon slices, cooked crisp and crumbled | 3 | 3 |
| Linguine pasta, broken into 1 inch (2.5 cm) lengths before measuring | 1 cup | 250 mL |
| Diced cooked chicken | 1½ cups | 375 mL |
| Salt | ¼ tsp. | 1 mL |

Put chicken stock, carrot, celery, onion and bacon into large pot or Dutch oven. Stir. Bring to a boil. Cover. Cook until vegetables are tender.

Add pasta, chicken and salt. Boil, uncovered, for about 15 minutes until pasta is tender. Makes 8 cups (2 L).

*1 cup (250 mL): 120 Calories; 2.9 g Total Fat; 886 mg Sodium; 12 g Protein; 11 g Carbohydrate; 1 g Dietary Fiber*

## CHICKEN SOUP

*This home-style soup is so colorful and inviting.*

| Water | 2½ cups | 625 mL |
|---|---|---|
| Boneless, skinless chicken breast half, diced | ¼ lb. | 113 g |
| Finely diced or sliced carrot | ¼ cup | 60 mL |
| Thinly sliced celery | ¼ cup | 60 mL |
| Parsley flakes | ½ tsp. | 2 mL |
| Chicken bouillon powder | 1 tsp. | 5 mL |
| Salt | ¼ tsp. | 1 mL |
| Pepper | ⅛ tsp. | 0.5 mL |
| Spaghetti, broken into 1 inch (2.5 cm) pieces before measuring | ¼ cup | 60 mL |

Measure first 8 ingredients into large saucepan. Bring to a boil, stirring often. Cover. Boil slowly for 30 minutes.

Add spaghetti. Cover. Boil slowly for about 15 minutes until spaghetti is cooked. Makes 2¼ cups (560 mL).

*1 cup (250 mL): 117 Calories; 1.1 g Total Fat; 644 mg Sodium; 14 g Protein; 12 g Carbohydrate; 1 g Dietary Fiber*

*To strengthen flavor of soup bases, chicken bouillon cubes or powder may be added. If using bones to make soup, browning bones before placing in slow cooker also adds to the flavor. You may choose to cook bones without the vegetables.*

# CHICKEN RICE SOUP

*At last, chicken soup with lots of chicken.*

| | | |
|---|---|---|
| Boneless, skinless chicken breast halves (about 2) | ¹⁄₂ lb. | 225 g |
| Whole chicken legs, skin removed | 2 | 2 |
| Small bay leaf | 1 | 1 |
| Vegetable bouillon powder | 1 tbsp. | 15 mL |
| Water | 6 cups | 1.5 L |
| Chopped celery | 1 cup | 250 mL |
| Medium carrot, diced | 1 | 1 |
| Chopped onion | 1¹⁄₂ cups | 375 mL |
| Cans of diced tomatoes (14 oz., 398 mL, each), with juice | 2 | 2 |
| Salt | ¹⁄₂ tsp. | 2 mL |
| Pepper, sprinkle | | |
| Uncooked long grain white rice | ¹⁄₂ cup | 125 mL |
| Parsley flakes | 1 tsp. | 5 mL |

Combine chicken, bay leaf, bouillon powder and water in large pot or Dutch oven. Bring to a boil. Skim off foam. Cook, uncovered, for about 30 minutes until chicken is tender. Remove chicken. Discard bones and bay leaf. Cut chicken into bite-size pieces. Return to pot.

Add next 6 ingredients. Cook, uncovered, for 20 minutes.

Add rice and parsley. Cook for 15 to 20 minutes until rice is tender. Makes 8¹⁄₂ cups (2.1 L).

*1 cup (250 mL):* 148 Calories; 2 g Total Fat; 586 mg Sodium; 15 g Protein; 18 g Carbohydrate; 2 g Dietary Fiber

1. Shrimp Chowder, page 104
2. Broccoli Cheese Soup, page 92
3. Exotic Soup, page 95

Props Courtesy Of: Le Gnome, The Bay

# Turkey Soup

*An old-fashioned thick, full-bodied soup. For chunkier soup, vegetables can be diced. Make ahead and freeze, or store, covered, in refrigerator for up to three days.*

| | | |
|---|---|---|
| Turkey wings, skin removed | 2 | 2 |
| Chopped onion | 1 cup | 250 mL |
| Chopped celery | 1/3 cup | 75 mL |
| Grated carrot | 1 cup | 250 mL |
| Grated potato | 1 cup | 250 mL |
| Thinly sliced cabbage, lightly packed | 1 cup | 250 mL |
| Water | 6 cups | 1.5 L |
| Chicken bouillon powder | 1 tbsp. | 15 mL |
| Salt | 1 tsp. | 5 mL |
| Pepper | 1/4 tsp. | 1 mL |

Place all 10 ingredients in large pot or Dutch oven. Bring to a boil, stirring occasionally. Cover. Boil slowly for 30 minutes. Remove wings. Cut off meat and discard bones. Chop turkey. Return to pot. Makes 6 cups (1.5 L).

*1 cup (250 mL): 81 Calories; 0.7 g Total Fat; 815 mg Sodium; 8 g Protein; 10 g Carbohydrate; 2 g Dietary Fiber*

# Turkey Vegetable Soup

*Made from the carcass and leftover turkey. Feeds a crowd or fills a freezer.*

| | | |
|---|---|---|
| Turkey carcass, broken up | 1 | 1 |
| Water | 14 cups | 3.5 L |
| Bay leaves | 2 | 2 |
| Salt | 1 tbsp. | 15 mL |
| Pepper | 3/4 tsp. | 4 mL |
| Granulated sugar | 1 tsp. | 5 mL |
| Medium carrots, sliced | 3 | 3 |
| Large onion, chopped | 1 | 1 |
| Celery ribs, sliced | 6 | 6 |
| Chicken bouillon powder | 1 tbsp. | 15 mL |
| Parsley flakes | 1 tbsp. | 15 mL |
| Dried thyme | 1/2 tsp. | 2 mL |
| Uncooked long grain white rice | 1/2 cup | 125 mL |
| Chopped cooked turkey | 2 cups | 500 mL |

Put turkey carcass, water, bay leaves, salt, pepper and sugar into large stockpot or Dutch oven. Stir. Bring to a boil. Cover. Simmer for 2 hours. Remove carcass. Discard bay leaves. Return any bits of meat to pot. Discard bones.

Add remaining 8 ingredients. Stir. Bring to a boil. Cover. Simmer for at least 30 minutes until all vegetables are cooked. Taste for seasoning. Add a bit more water if too thick. Makes about 15 cups (3.7 L).

*1 cup (250 mL): 131 Calories; 2.8 g Total Fat; 939 mg Sodium; 15 g Protein; 10 g Carbohydrate; 1 g Dietary Fiber*

1. Fish Chowder, page 102

Props Courtesy Of: Le Gnome, Scona Clayworks, X/S Wares

# Cream Soups

*T*hese recipes offer velvety, soothing flavors to warm the soul. Creamy soups also feature an elegant side to their presentation, making them an excellent dish to serve at a dinner party. Just before presenting your soup, sprinkle the center of the surface with toppings such as chopped green onion, grated cheese, a spoonful of sour cream or a few croutons for added decoration.

## BROCCOLI CHEESE SOUP

*Colorful, with carrot showing through.*

| | | |
|---|---|---|
| **Thinly sliced carrot** | 1 cup | 250 mL |
| **Water** | 2 tbsp. | 30 mL |
| **Frozen chopped broccoli** | 10 oz. | 300 g |
| **Milk** | 2½ cups | 625 mL |
| **All-purpose flour** | ¼ cup | 60 mL |
| **Chicken bouillon powder** | 2 tsp. | 10 mL |
| **Salt** | ½ tsp. | 2 mL |
| **Pepper** | ¼ tsp. | 1 mL |
| **Water** | 1 cup | 250 mL |
| **Grated medium Cheddar cheese** | 1 cup | 250 mL |

Place carrot and first amount of water in 2 quart (2 L) microwave-safe casserole. Cover. Microwave on high (100%) for 3 minutes. Stir. Cover. Microwave on high (100%) for about 3 minutes until tender.

Add broccoli. Cover. Microwave on high (100%) for about 3 minutes. Stir. Cover. Microwave on high (100%) for about 2 minutes until tender. Add milk. Stir.

Combine flour, bouillon powder, salt and pepper in small bowl. Add ½ of second amount of water. Mix until smooth. Add remaining ½ of water. Pour over carrot mixture. Cover. Microwave on high (100%) for about 3 minutes. Stir. Cover. Microwave on high (100%) for about 8 minutes, stirring at 1 minute intervals, until mixture is boiling and thickened.

Add cheese. Stir until cheese is melted. Makes 4¾ cups (1.2 L).

*1 cup (250 mL): 215 Calories; 10.2 g Total Fat; 806 mg Sodium; 14 g Protein; 18 g Carbohydrate; 3 g Dietary Fiber*

Pictured on page 89.

## ROASTED ONION AND GARLIC BISQUE

*Use Vidalia or Walla Walla sweet onions. To freeze this soup, make without the evaporated milk. Add the milk once the soup is thawed. Heat and serve.*

| | | |
|---|---|---|
| Large garlic bulb | 1 | 1 |
| Large white onions, cut into wedges | 4-5 | 4-5 |
| Olive oil (or cooking spray) | 2 tsp. | 10 mL |
| Olive oil (or cooking spray) | 1 tsp. | 5 mL |
| Medium leeks (white and tender green parts only), thinly sliced | 2 | 2 |
| All-purpose flour | 2 tbsp. | 30 mL |
| Dried thyme | 1 tsp. | 5 mL |
| Salt | 1 tsp. | 5 mL |
| Condensed chicken broth (10 oz., 284 mL, each) | 2 | 2 |
| Dry (or alcohol-free) white wine | 1/3 cup | 75 mL |
| Cans of skim evaporated milk (13½ oz., 385 mL, each) | 2 | 2 |
| Non-fat sour cream, for garnish | | |

Remove loose outer covering on garlic without separating cloves. Place garlic and onion on lightly greased baking sheet. Lightly brush surface of garlic and onion wedges with first amount of olive oil. Bake in 350°F (175°C) oven for 1 hour. Cool.

Heat second amount of olive oil in large pot or Dutch oven. Sauté leeks for 20 minutes until soft and golden. Sprinkle with flour, thyme and salt. Stir well. Stir in chicken broth.

Squeeze garlic pulp into blender. Add onion. Process. Gradually add white wine, processing until smooth. Pour into leek mixture. Simmer for 30 minutes. Remove from heat.

Stir in evaporated milk. Heat gently until hot. Do not boil.

Garnish with dollop of sour cream. Makes 8 cups (2 L).

*1 cup (250 mL): 190 Calories; 3 g Total Fat; 941 mg Sodium; 3 g Protein; 27 g Carbohydrate; 2 g Dietary Fiber*

## ASPARAGUS SOUP

*A smooth soup. Just the right consistency.*

| | | |
|---|---|---|
| Water | 1 cup | 250 mL |
| Fresh asparagus, cut up | ½ lb. | 225 g |
| Margarine | 2 tbsp. | 30 mL |
| All-purpose flour | 2 tbsp. | 30 mL |
| Salt | ½ tsp. | 2 mL |
| Pepper | 1/8 tsp. | 0.5 mL |
| Milk | 2 cups | 500 mL |

Place water and asparagus in medium saucepan. Cover. Cook for about 10 minutes until tender. Do not drain. Pour into blender.

Melt margarine in small saucepan. Mix in flour, salt and pepper. Stir in milk until mixture is boiling and thickened. Add to blender. Purée. Return to medium saucepan to heat through. Makes 3¼ cups (800 mL).

*1 cup (250 mL): 190 Calories; 11.3 g Total Fat; 619 mg Sodium; 8 g Protein; 15 g Carbohydrate; 2 g Dietary Fiber*

## PUMPKIN SOUP

*The color and flavor of pumpkin.*

| | | |
|---|---|---|
| Margarine | 1 tbsp. | 15 mL |
| Chopped onion | 1 cup | 250 mL |
| Can of diced tomatoes, with juice | 14 oz. | 398 mL |
| Can of pumpkin, without added spices (or same quantity fresh, cooked and mashed) | 14 oz. | 398 mL |
| Instant vegetable stock mix | 2 tbsp. | 30 mL |
| Water | 2 cups | 500 mL |
| Milk | 2 cups | 500 mL |
| Salt | 1½ tsp. | 7 mL |
| Pepper | ⅛-¼ tsp. | 0.5-1 mL |

Melt margarine in large pot or Dutch oven. Add onion. Sauté until soft.

Add remaining 7 ingredients. Heat, stirring often, until very hot. Do not boil or mixture might curdle. Makes 7 cups (1.75 L).

*1 cup (250 mL): 106 Calories; 3.2 g Total Fat; 914 mg Sodium; 2 g Protein; 12 g Carbohydrate; 2 g Dietary Fiber*

Pictured on page 72.

**Variation:** Add ⅛ to ¼ tsp. (0.5 to 1 mL) ground thyme for a great flavor.

## CAULIFLOWER SOUP

*Smooth and white with green flakes showing. Good soup.*

| | | |
|---|---|---|
| Water | 1 cup | 250 mL |
| Chopped cauliflower | 2½ cups | 625 mL |
| Chopped onion | ⅓ cup | 75 mL |
| Chicken bouillon powder | ½ tsp. | 2 mL |
| Salt | ⅛ tsp. | 0.5 mL |
| Pepper | 1/16 tsp. | 0.5 mL |
| Milk | 1 cup | 250 mL |
| Parsley flakes | 1 tsp. | 5 mL |

Combine first 6 ingredients in medium saucepan. Stir. Cover. Cook for 10 to 12 minutes until tender. Do not drain.

Stir in milk and parsley flakes. Pour into blender. Process until smooth. Return to saucepan. Heat through. Makes 3 cups (750 mL).

*1 cup (250 mL): 73 Calories; 1.9 g Total Fat; 286 mg Sodium; 5 g Protein; 10 g Carbohydrate; 2 g Dietary Fiber*

**CAULIFLOWER CHEESE SOUP:** Stir in 2 tbsp. (30 mL) grated sharp Cheddar cheese to melt or add to ingredients in blender.

*To prevent a cream soup from scorching, keep it hot over warm water in the top of a double boiler until ready to serve.*

# EXOTIC SOUP

*No one will be able to guess what kind of soup this is because the curry flavor is subtle. Good served with or without it.*

| | | |
|---|---|---|
| Condensed cream of asparagus soup | 10 oz. | 284 mL |
| Condensed cream of chicken soup | 10 oz. | 284 mL |
| Condensed beef broth | 10 oz. | 284 mL |
| Non-fat sour cream | 1 cup | 250 mL |
| Curry powder | 1/4 tsp. | 1 mL |
| Chopped chives, for garnish | | |

Process first 5 ingredients in blender. Pour into medium saucepan. Heat, stirring often, until very hot.

Sprinkle individual servings with chives. Makes 4 1/2 cups (1.1 L).

*1 cup (250 mL): 135 Calories; 6.6 g Total Fat; 1357 mg Sodium; 6 g Protein; 14 g Carbohydrate; trace Dietary Fiber*

Pictured on page 89.

# GREEN CHILI SOUP

*Very light green in color with a mild chili flavor. Easy to double. Make the day before and reheat just before serving.*

| | | |
|---|---|---|
| Water | 1 cup | 250 mL |
| Finely chopped onion | 1/4 cup | 60 mL |
| Light cream cheese, softened, cut up | 4 oz. | 125 g |
| Non-fat sour cream | 1/2 cup | 125 mL |
| Can of diced green chilies, with liquid | 4 oz. | 114 mL |
| Garlic powder | 1/8 tsp. | 0.5 mL |
| Chicken bouillon powder | 1 tsp. | 5 mL |
| Milk | 1 cup | 250 mL |
| Skim evaporated milk | 1/2 cup | 125 mL |
| Salt | 1/8 tsp. | 0.5 mL |
| Pepper, sprinkle | | |

Place water and onion in medium saucepan. Cook until onion is soft. Cool. Pour into blender.

Add cream cheese, sour cream, green chilies with liquid, garlic powder and bouillon powder to onion mixture. Process until smooth. Return to saucepan.

Add both milks, salt and pepper. Heat through. Makes 4 cups (1 L).

*1 cup (250 mL): 137 Calories; 6.1 g Total Fat; 825 mg Sodium; 9 g Protein; 12 g Carbohydrate; trace Dietary Fiber*

*Pour leftover soup into ice cube trays and freeze. Remove cubes and store in plastic bags. To use, just thaw as many cubes as needed.*

## SWEET PEPPER SOUP
*A colorful and delicious soup.*

| | | |
|---|---|---|
| Chopped red pepper (about 10 medium) | 7 cups | 1.75 L |
| Chopped onion | 2 cups | 500 mL |
| Chicken bouillon powder | 1/4 cup | 60 mL |
| Water | 2 cups | 500 mL |
| Milk | 3 1/2 cups | 875 mL |
| Salt | 1 tsp. | 5 mL |
| Pepper | 1/4 tsp. | 1 mL |
| Ground thyme | 1/4 tsp. | 1 mL |
| Cornstarch | 2 tbsp. | 30 mL |
| Water | 3 tbsp. | 50 mL |

Combine first 4 ingredients in large saucepan. Cover. Simmer until tender. Do not drain. Cool slightly. Pour into blender. Process.

Combine milk, salt, pepper and thyme in same saucepan. Bring to a boil. Add red pepper mixture. Return to a boil.

Mix cornstarch and second amount of water in small bowl. Stir into soup until boiling and thickened. Makes a generous 8 cups (2 L).

*1 cup (250 mL): 110 Calories; 2.2 g Total Fat; 1375 mg Sodium; 6 g Protein; 18 g Carbohydrate; 2 g Dietary Fiber*

*Store fresh peppers, wrapped loosely in a tea towel, in a ventilated plastic bag in the refrigerator.*

## TOMATO CREAM SOUP
*A tomato soup with vegetables.*

| | | |
|---|---|---|
| Margarine | 3 tbsp. | 50 mL |
| Chopped onion | 1 cup | 250 mL |
| Diced carrot | 1 cup | 250 mL |
| Medium tomatoes | 4 | 4 |
| Sliced celery | 1/2 cup | 125 mL |
| Condensed chicken broth (10 oz., 284 mL, each) | 2 | 2 |
| Tomato sauce | 7 1/2 oz. | 213 mL |
| Granulated sugar | 1 tbsp. | 15 mL |
| Whole black peppercorns | 12 | 12 |
| Parsley flakes | 1/2 tsp. | 2 mL |
| Salt | 2 tsp. | 10 mL |
| Beef bouillon cube (1/5 oz., 6 g) | 1 | 1 |
| Boiling water | 1 1/4 cups | 300 mL |
| Light cream | 3/4 cup | 175 mL |

Melt margarine in large saucepan. Add onion and carrot. Sauté until soft.

Dip tomatoes into boiling water for about 1 minute until they peel easily. Cut up. Add to saucepan. Add next 7 ingredients. Stir.

Dissolve bouillon cube in boiling water in cup. Add to soup. Stir. Cover. Simmer for 30 minutes.

Add cream when ready to serve. Stir to heat through. Do not boil. Pour into soup bowls. Makes about 8 cups (2 L).

*1 cup (250 mL): 136 Calories; 8 g Total Fat; 1524 mg Sodium; 6 g Protein; 12 g Carbohydrate; 2 g Dietary Fiber*

# CREAM OF GARLIC SOUP

*A creamy foolproof version of an unusual soup. For garlic lovers. Add as many garlic cloves as you dare. Garnish with chopped chives.*

| | | |
|---|---|---|
| **Garlic cloves, minced** | 4-8 | 4-8 |
| **Margarine** | 3 tbsp. | 50 mL |
| **All-purpose flour** | 3 tbsp. | 50 mL |
| **Condensed chicken broth (10 oz., 284 mL, each)** | 2 | 2 |
| **Soup cans of milk (10 oz., 284 mL, each)** | 2 | 2 |
| **Paprika** | ½ tsp. | 2 mL |

Sauté garlic in margarine in medium saucepan until golden.

Mix in flour. Add chicken broth, stirring until boiling and thickened. Add milk and paprika. Stir. Simmer for about 5 minutes until garlic is soft and cooked. Makes about 4½ cups (1.1 L).

*1 cup (250 mL): 190 Calories; 10.7 g Total Fat; 996 mg Sodium; 11 g Protein; 12 g Carbohydrate; trace Dietary Fiber*

Pictured on page 54.

# CREAM OF CARROT SOUP

*Smooth and soothing. A sure hit.*

| | | |
|---|---|---|
| **Margarine** | ¼ cup | 60 mL |
| **Medium onions, chopped** | 2 | 2 |
| **Garlic clove, minced** | 1 | 1 |
| **Medium potatoes, diced** | 3 | 3 |
| **Medium carrots, diced** | 4 | 4 |
| **Chicken stock** | 5 cups | 1.25 L |
| **Bay leaf** | 1 | 1 |
| **Ground thyme** | ¼-½ tsp. | 1-2 mL |
| **Pepper** | ¼ tsp. | 1 mL |

Melt margarine in large saucepan. Add onion and garlic. Sauté until clear and soft.

Add remaining 6 ingredients, using smaller amount of thyme. Bring to a boil. Cover. Simmer until vegetables are tender. Discard bay leaf. Add more thyme if desired. Makes 8½ cups (2.1 L).

*1 cup (250 mL): 114 Calories; 6 g Total Fat; 512 mg Sodium; 2 g Protein; 14 g Carbohydrate; 2 g Dietary Fiber*

# VELVET POTATO SOUP

*A mild cream soup. Excellent starter for a sit-down dinner party. Cook and mash potatoes the day before, then you only have ten minutes preparation time left.*

| | | |
|---|---|---|
| **Warm mashed cooked potato** | 2 cups | 500 mL |
| **All-purpose flour** | 1 tbsp. | 15 mL |
| **Milk** | 3 cups | 750 mL |
| **Parsley flakes** | 1 tsp. | 5 mL |
| **Onion flakes** | 1 tsp. | 5 mL |
| **Celery salt** | ¾ tsp. | 4 mL |
| **Pepper (white is best)** | ⅛-¼ tsp. | 0.5-1 mL |
| **Chicken bouillon powder** | 1½ tsp. | 7 mL |
| **Chopped chives, sprinkle** | | |

Mash potato again with flour in large saucepan. Add next 6 ingredients. Heat, stirring often, until boiling and smooth. Simmer for 5 minutes.

Garnish with chives. Makes 5 cups (1.25 L).

*1 cup (250 mL): 169 Calories; 2 g Total Fat; 485 mg Sodium; 8 g Protein; 31 g Carbohydrate; 2 g Dietary Fiber*

## MUSHROOM SOUP

*This dark beige soup contains bread crumbs which slightly thicken it.*

| | | |
|---|---|---|
| Sliced fresh mushrooms | 3 cups | 750 mL |
| Margarine | 1 tbsp. | 15 mL |
| Water | 1 cup | 250 mL |
| Can of skim evaporated milk | 13$\frac{1}{2}$ oz. | 385 mL |
| Chicken bouillon powder | 2 tsp. | 10 mL |
| Paprika | $\frac{1}{4}$ tsp. | 1 mL |
| Garlic powder | $\frac{1}{4}$ tsp. | 1 mL |
| Salt | $\frac{1}{4}$ tsp. | 1 mL |
| Pepper, sprinkle | | |
| White (or alcohol-free) wine | 2 tbsp. | 30 mL |
| Dry bread crumbs | $\frac{1}{4}$ cup | 60 mL |

Combine mushrooms and margarine in 8 cup (2 L) microwave-safe liquid measure. Cover with plastic wrap. Microwave on high (100%) for 1 minute. Stir. Cover. Microwave on high (100%) for about 3 minutes until soft.

Add next 9 ingredients. Stir. Process in blender. Return to measure. Cook, uncovered, on high (100%) for about 3 minutes until mixture starts to boil. Microwave on medium-low (30%) for about 5 minutes until flavors are blended. Makes 4 cups (1 L).

*1 cup (250 mL): 159 Calories; 3.8 g Total Fat; 703 mg Sodium; 10 g Protein; 20 g Carbohydrate; 1 g Dietary Fiber*

Pictured on page 71.

## CREAMY CHICKEN SOUP

*Creamy good with the unusual addition of cheese.*

| | | |
|---|---|---|
| Diced potato | 2$\frac{1}{2}$ cups | 625 mL |
| Chopped onion | $\frac{1}{2}$ cup | 125 mL |
| Chopped carrot | $\frac{1}{2}$ cup | 125 mL |
| Chopped celery | $\frac{1}{2}$ cup | 125 mL |
| Boiling water | | |
| Condensed cream of mushroom soup | 10 oz. | 284 mL |
| Milk | 2$\frac{1}{2}$ cups | 625 mL |
| Diced cooked chicken | 1 cup | 250 mL |
| Worcestershire sauce | $\frac{1}{4}$ tsp. | 1 mL |
| Parsley flakes | $\frac{1}{4}$ tsp. | 1 mL |
| Salt | $\frac{1}{4}$ tsp. | 1 mL |
| Pepper | $\frac{1}{8}$ tsp. | 0.5 mL |
| Ground thyme | $\frac{1}{8}$ tsp. | 0.5 mL |
| Grated medium or sharp Cheddar cheese | 1 cup | 250 mL |

Cook potato, onion, carrot and celery in boiling water in large saucepan until tender. Drain. Mash.

Add next 8 ingredients. Stir. Heat to simmer.

Add cheese. Stir until melted. Makes 6$\frac{2}{3}$ cups (1.65 L).

*1 cup (250 mL): 262 Calories; 11.3 g Total Fat; 668 mg Sodium; 17 g Protein; 23 g Carbohydrate; 2 g Dietary Fiber*

# HEARTY ZUCCHINI CHOWDER

*Thick and creamy with a subtle dill taste. Only takes about 30 minutes to prepare.*

| | | |
|---|---|---|
| Small garlic clove, minced | 1 | 1 |
| Chopped onion | 1 cup | 250 mL |
| Chopped celery | 1/2 cup | 125 mL |
| Chopped green pepper | 1/2 cup | 125 mL |
| Margarine | 1 tsp. | 5 mL |
| Grated zucchini, with peel | 2 cups | 500 mL |
| Diced potato | 2 cups | 500 mL |
| Water | 6 cups | 1.5 L |
| Vegetable (or chicken) bouillon powder | 2 tbsp. | 30 mL |
| Uncooked tubetti (very small) pasta | 1 cup | 250 mL |
| Dill weed | 1 tsp. | 5 mL |
| Salt | 1/2 tsp. | 2 mL |
| Pepper | 1/8-1/4 tsp. | 0.5-1 mL |
| All-purpose flour | 3 tbsp. | 50 mL |
| Skim evaporated milk | 1 cup | 250 mL |

Sauté garlic, onion, celery and green pepper in margarine in large pot or Dutch oven for about 3 minutes until vegetables are soft.

Add next 4 ingredients. Simmer, partially covered, for 20 minutes.

Stir in pasta, dill weed, salt and pepper. Simmer for 10 to 15 minutes, stirring occasionally, until pasta is tender but firm.

Whisk flour and evaporated milk together in small bowl until smooth. Add to soup, stirring continually, until mixture boils. Makes 9 cups (2.25 L).

*1 cup (250 mL): 126 Calories; 1 g Total Fat; 598 mg Sodium; 6 g Protein; 24 g Carbohydrate; 2 g Dietary Fiber*

# CORN CHOWDER

*Serve this for rave reviews.*

| | | |
|---|---|---|
| Diced potato | 3 cups | 750 mL |
| Chopped celery | 1 cup | 250 mL |
| Grated carrot | 1 cup | 250 mL |
| Chopped onion | 1 cup | 250 mL |
| Water | 1 cup | 250 mL |
| Bacon slices, cooked crisp and crumbled | 6 | 6 |
| Milk | 2 1/4 cups | 560 mL |
| Can of skim evaporated milk | 13 1/2 oz. | 385 mL |
| All-purpose flour | 1/4 cup | 60 mL |
| Salt | 1 tsp. | 5 mL |
| Pepper | 1/2 tsp. | 2 mL |
| Can of cream-style corn | 14 oz. | 398 mL |

Cook potato, celery, carrot and onion slowly in water in large pot or Dutch oven until tender. Add a bit more water if needed to keep from burning. Drain well. Remove vegetables to large bowl.

Add bacon to cooked vegetables.

Gradually whisk both milks, flour, salt and pepper together in small bowl. Pour into pot. Stir until boiling and thickened.

Add corn and vegetable mixture to pot. Stir to heat through. Makes 10 cups (2.5 L).

*1 cup (250 mL): 210 Calories; 6 g Total Fat; 652 mg Sodium; 11 g Protein; 30 g Carbohydrate; 2 g Dietary Fiber*

# Fish & Seafood Soups

*H*ere's a delicious way to include that healthy serving of fish we should be getting every week. Seafood lovers will adore these classic, mouth-watering recipes. Even those stubborn family members who are reluctant to try fish or seafood will change their minds once they sample one of these superb recipes.

## SHRIMP AND MUSHROOM SOUP

*A delicious combination of shrimp and mushrooms. Makes a great starter soup for a sit-down dinner. Garnish with shrimp.*

| | | |
|---|---|---|
| Margarine | 1 tbsp. | 15 mL |
| Finely chopped onion | ⅓ cup | 75 mL |
| Chopped fresh mushrooms | 2 cups | 500 mL |
| All-purpose flour | ¼ cup | 60 mL |
| Salt | ½ tsp. | 2 mL |
| Dry mustard | ½ tsp. | 2 mL |
| Garlic salt | ¼ tsp. | 1 mL |
| Pepper | ⅛ tsp. | 0.5 mL |
| Can of skim evaporated milk | 13½ oz. | 385 mL |
| Milk | 1⅓ cups | 325 mL |
| Water | 1 cup | 250 mL |
| Sherry (or alcohol-free sherry), optional | 1 tbsp. | 15 mL |
| Cans of broken (or cocktail) shrimp (4 oz., 113 g, each), with liquid | 2 | 2 |

Melt margarine in large non-stick frying pan. Add onion and mushrooms. Sauté until onion is soft and moisture is evaporated.

Mix in next 5 ingredients.

Stir in both milks and water until boiling and thickened. Add sherry. Stir.

Add shrimp with liquid. Heat through. Makes about 5 cups (1.25 L).

*1 cup (250 mL): 206 Calories; 4.4 g Total Fat; 577 mg Sodium; 20 g Protein; 21 g Carbohydrate; 1 g Dietary Fiber*

# MANHATTAN CLAM CHOWDER

*A good variation of clam chowder. Reddish orange in color with a very good taste.*

| | | |
|---|---|---|
| Bacon slices, diced | 4 | 4 |
| Chopped onion | 1 cup | 250 mL |
| | | |
| Medium potatoes, diced | 2 | 2 |
| Can of diced tomatoes, with juice | 14 oz. | 398 mL |
| Finely diced celery | 1 cup | 250 mL |
| Chicken bouillon powder | 1 tbsp. | 15 mL |
| Salt | 1/2 tsp. | 2 mL |
| Pepper | 1/4 tsp. | 1 mL |
| Ground thyme | 1/4 tsp. | 1 mL |
| Cayenne pepper (optional) | 1/8 tsp. | 0.5 mL |
| Water | 3 cups | 750 mL |
| | | |
| All-purpose flour | 1/4 cup | 60 mL |
| Water | 1 cup | 250 mL |
| | | |
| Can of baby clams, with juice, chopped | 5 oz. | 142 g |

Fry bacon and onion in large pot or Dutch oven until bacon is cooked and onion is clear. Drain.

Add next 9 ingredients. Bring to a boil. Cover. Boil gently for about 25 minutes until vegetables are tender.

Mix flour and second amount of water in small bowl until smooth. Stir into potato mixture until boiling and thickened.

Add clams with juice. Stir. Heat through. Makes 7 1/3 cups (1.8 L).

*1 cup (250 mL): 154 Calories; 7.8 g Total Fat; 707 mg Sodium; 6 g Protein; 15 g Carbohydrate; 2 g Dietary Fiber*

# NEW ENGLAND CLAM CHOWDER

*Dark cream soup with vegetables.*

| | | |
|---|---|---|
| Medium potatoes, diced | 3 | 3 |
| Finely chopped celery | 1/2 cup | 125 mL |
| Grated carrot | 1 cup | 250 mL |
| Water | 1 cup | 250 mL |
| | | |
| Bacon slices, diced | 3 | 3 |
| Chopped onion | 1 1/2 cups | 375 mL |
| | | |
| Margarine | 3 tbsp. | 50 mL |
| All-purpose flour | 1/2 cup | 125 mL |
| Salt | 1 tsp. | 5 mL |
| Pepper | 1/8 tsp. | 0.5 mL |
| Milk | 2 cups | 500 mL |
| | | |
| Can of skim evaporated milk | 13 1/2 oz. | 385 mL |
| Cream-style corn | 1/2 cup | 125 mL |
| Can of baby clams, with juice, chopped | 5 oz. | 142 g |

Put first 4 ingredients into large saucepan. Cover. Simmer for about 20 minutes until tender. Do not drain.

Fry bacon and onion in large frying pan until bacon is cooked and onion is clear. Do not drain.

Add margarine, flour, salt and pepper. Mix. Stir in milk until boiling and thickened. Stir into potato mixture in saucepan.

Add evaporated milk, corn and clams with juice. Heat slowly, stirring often, until steaming hot, but not boiling. Makes 8 cups (2 L).

*1 cup (250 mL): 265 Calories; 10.6 g Total Fat; 661 mg Sodium; 12 g Protein; 31 g Carbohydrate; 2 g Dietary Fiber*

## CRAB SOUP

*Chunky soup with colorful ingredients. So tasty.*

| | | |
|---|---|---|
| Can of stewed tomatoes, with juice | 14 oz. | 398 mL |
| Chopped onion | 1 cup | 250 mL |
| Chopped celery | ½ cup | 125 mL |
| Grated potato | 1½ cups | 375 mL |
| Grated carrot | ½ cup | 125 mL |
| Water | 3 cups | 750 mL |
| Milk | ½ cup | 125 mL |
| All-purpose flour | ¼ cup | 60 mL |
| Chicken bouillon powder | 1 tbsp. | 15 mL |
| Salt | 1 tsp. | 5 mL |
| Pepper | ⅛-¼ tsp. | 0.5-1 mL |
| Can of skim evaporated milk | 13½ oz. | 385 mL |
| Can of crabmeat, with liquid, cartilage removed, flaked | 4¼ oz. | 120 g |

Combine first 6 ingredients in large saucepan. Cover. Cook until vegetables are tender.

Measure next 5 ingredients into small bowl. Stir until no lumps remain. Stir into tomato mixture until boiling and thickened.

Add evaporated milk and crabmeat. Heat slowly, stirring often, until steaming hot, but not boiling. Makes 8 cups (2 L).

*1 cup (250 mL): 127 Calories; 0.8 g Total Fat; 905 mg Sodium; 9 g Protein; 22 g Carbohydrate; 2 g Dietary Fiber*

**TUNA SOUP:** Use 1 can tuna (6½ oz., 184 g) with liquid, instead of crabmeat.

## FISH CHOWDER

*Directly from the Atlantic provinces.*

| | | |
|---|---|---|
| Margarine | ½ cup | 125 mL |
| Chopped onion | 1 cup | 250 mL |
| Diced celery | ½ cup | 125 mL |
| Green pepper, diced | 1 | 1 |
| Diced potato | 1 cup | 250 mL |
| Boiling water | 1½ cups | 375 mL |
| Salt | 1½ tsp. | 7 mL |
| Pepper | ⅛ tsp. | 0.5 mL |
| Bay leaf | 1 | 1 |
| Haddock fillets (or combination of haddock and lobster), cut bite size | 2 lbs. | 900 g |
| Skim evaporated milk | 2 cups | 500 mL |
| Granulated sugar | 1 tsp. | 5 mL |
| Freshly ground pepper, sprinkle | | |
| Chopped fresh parsley, for garnish | | |

Melt margarine in large saucepan. Add onion, celery and green pepper. Sauté until soft.

Add next 5 ingredients. Cover. Cook until potato is just tender. Do not overcook. Discard bay leaf.

Add fillet pieces. Cook for about 5 minutes until fish flakes when tested with fork.

Stir in evaporated milk and sugar. Heat slowly, stirring often, until steaming hot, but not boiling.

Sprinkle individual servings with pepper and garnish with parsley. Makes 8 cups (2 L).

*1 cup (250 mL): 289 Calories; 13.3 g Total Fat; 815 mg Sodium; 27 g Protein; 15 g Carbohydrate; 1 g Dietary Fiber*

Pictured on page 90.

# LOBSTER CHOWDER FEED

*Start a Christmas Eve tradition. Serves a large group—but be prepared for seconds. Great with a basket of warm baking powder biscuits.*

| | | |
|---|---|---|
| Margarine | ½ cup | 125 mL |
| Chopped onion | 3 cups | 750 mL |
| Diced celery | 2 cups | 500 mL |
| Small green peppers, diced | 2 | 2 |
| All-purpose flour | ½ cup | 125 mL |
| Boiling water | 4 cups | 1 L |
| Diced potato | 5 cups | 1.25 L |
| Salt | 3½ tsp. | 17 mL |
| Pepper | ½ tsp. | 2 mL |
| Margarine | ¼ cup | 60 mL |
| Cans of frozen lobster (11.3 oz., 320 mL, each), thawed | 2 | 2 |
| Boiling water | 1 cup | 250 mL |
| Scallops, halved if large | 1 lb. | 454 g |
| Haddock fillets, cut bite size | 2 lbs. | 900 g |
| Cans of skim evaporated milk (13½ oz., 385 mL, each) | 2 | 2 |
| Milk | 3 cups | 750 mL |

Melt first amount of margarine in medium frying pan. Add onion, celery and green pepper. Sauté until tender.

Sprinkle flour over vegetables. Mix in well.

Put first amount of boiling water, potato, salt and pepper into large pot or Dutch oven. Stir. Cover. Cook until potato is just tender. Add onion mixture.

Melt second amount of margarine in same frying pan. Add lobster. Sauté just long enough for red color from lobster to go into margarine. Add to potato mixture.

Put second amount of boiling water and scallops into small saucepan. Cook for 3 to 5 minutes until opaque. Do not drain. Add to potato mixture.

Add haddock to potato mixture. Stir. Cook until fish turns white and flakes or falls apart.

Add both milks. Heat, stirring occasionally, until hot. Do not boil. Makes 6 quarts (6 L).

*1 cup (250 mL): 218 Calories; 7.2 g Total Fat; 693 mg Sodium; 21 g Protein; 17 g Carbohydrate; 1 g Dietary Fiber*

*If you have picky eaters in your family who don't like chunks of onion or green pepper in their soup, purée those ingredients in the blender before putting into the soup.*

## SHRIMP CHOWDER

*Chunky, rich and thick. Nice combination of shrimp and cheese. Light orange in color.*

| | | |
|---|---|---|
| Chopped onion | 2 cups | 500 mL |
| Margarine | 3 tbsp. | 50 mL |
| Diced potato | 3 cups | 750 mL |
| Water | 1¼ cups | 300 mL |
| Salt | ½ tsp. | 2 mL |
| Pepper | ⅛ tsp. | 0.5 mL |
| Milk | 1 cup | 250 mL |
| Pasteurized cheese loaf, cut up | 8 oz. | 250 g |
| Cans of broken shrimp (4 oz., 113 g, each), drained and rinsed | 2 | 2 |

Sauté onion in margarine in large saucepan until soft.

Add potato, water, salt and pepper. Cover. Cook until potato is tender. Do not drain. Mash about ½ of potato.

Add milk and cheese. Heat slowly, stirring often, until cheese is melted.

Add shrimp. Stir. Simmer to blend flavors. Makes 6 cups (1.5 L).

*1 cup (250 mL): 331 Calories; 17.4 g Total Fat; 1044 mg Sodium; 20 g Protein; 25 g Carbohydrate; 2 g Dietary Fiber*

Pictured on page 89.

## TUNA BISQUE

*A really good soup. Tasty and colorful.*

| | | |
|---|---|---|
| Condensed tomato soup | 10 oz. | 284 mL |
| Can of skim evaporated milk | 13½ oz. | 385 mL |
| Milk | ⅓ cup | 75 mL |
| Dried sweet basil | ½ tsp. | 2 mL |
| Can of tuna, drained and flaked | 6½ oz. | 184 g |
| Sherry (or alcohol-free sherry) | 2 tbsp. | 30 mL |

Combine first 4 ingredients in 4 cup (1 L) microwave-safe liquid measure. Stir well. Heat, uncovered, on high (100%) for about 7 minutes, stirring twice, until mixture starts to boil.

Add tuna and sherry. Stir. Heat on high (100%) for about 1½ minutes until heated through. Makes 4 cups (1 L).

*1 cup (250 mL): 198 Calories; 1.8 g Total Fat; 792 mg Sodium; 21 g Protein; 23 g Carbohydrate; 1 g Dietary Fiber*

Pictured on page 108.

*Simmer vinegar in a small saucepan to rid the house of odors, especially fish and seafood.*

# Pasta Soups

**H**ere is a collection of recipes guaranteed to become family favorites. If you want to have fun with these zesty and fanciful soups, try changing the kind of pasta you put into your recipes. Stars, swirls, and even colorful Christmas pasta, add whimsy and fun, appealing to the child in all of us. Avoid freezing these soups because frozen pasta will change in texture and become mushy.

## LENTIL AND PASTA SOUP

*A robust hearty soup with lots of texture. About 20 minutes preparation time.*

|  | | |
|---|---|---|
| Garlic cloves, minced | 2 | 2 |
| Finely chopped onion | 1 cup | 250 mL |
| Chopped celery | 1 cup | 250 mL |
| Olive oil | 2 tsp. | 10 mL |
| Water | 7 cups | 1.75 L |
| Beef (or chicken) bouillon powder | 2 tbsp. | 30 mL |
| Can of tomatoes, with juice, processed | 14 oz. | 398 mL |
| Thinly sliced carrot | 1½ cups | 375 mL |
| Green lentils | ¾ cup | 175 mL |
| Parsley flakes | 2 tsp. | 10 mL |
| Dried sweet basil | 1 tsp. | 5 mL |
| Salt | 1 tsp. | 5 mL |
| Ground oregano, just a pinch | | |
| Pepper, sprinkle | | |
| Uncooked tubetti (very small) pasta | 1 cup | 250 mL |

Sauté garlic, onion and celery in olive oil in large pot or Dutch oven until onion is soft.

Add next 10 ingredients. Bring mixture to a boil. Stir. Simmer, partially covered, for 30 minutes.

Stir in pasta. Simmer for 15 minutes. Makes 8 cups (2 L).

*1 cup (250 mL): 158 Calories; 2 g Total Fat; 893 mg Sodium; 8 g Protein; 28 g Carbohydrate; 4 g Dietary Fiber*

## LEMON PESTO SOUP

*A very refreshing soup. Only ten minutes preparation time.*

| | | |
|---|---|---|
| Condensed chicken broth (10 oz., 284 mL, each) | 3 | 3 |
| Water | 3 cups | 750 mL |
| Basil pesto | 1 tbsp. | 15 mL |
| Uncooked tubetti (very small) pasta | ¾ cup | 175 mL |
| Lemon juice | 2 tbsp. | 30 mL |
| Large eggs | 2 | 2 |
| Chopped fresh parsley | ¼ cup | 60 mL |
| Salt, just a pinch | | |
| Pepper, sprinkle | | |

Combine chicken broth, water and pesto in large saucepan. Bring to a boil.

Add pasta. Stir well. Simmer, uncovered, for 3 minutes.

Beat lemon juice and eggs together in small bowl. Remove some hot broth mixture with ladle and stir into egg mixture. Slowly add egg mixture to soup, stirring constantly. Remove from heat. Cover. Let stand for 5 minutes.

Stir in parsley, salt and pepper. Makes 7 cups (1.75 L).

*1 cup (250 mL): 135 Calories; 4.2 g Total Fat; 837 mg Sodium; 10 g Protein; 14 g Carbohydrate; 1 g Dietary Fiber*

**Variation:** Substitute chopped fresh mint for parsley.

*The easiest way to chop fresh herbs, such as parsley or sweet basil, is to use kitchen shears. Hold fresh herbs over a glass measure as you snip to accurately measure the amount.*

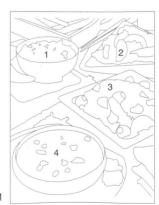

1. Noodles And Soup, page 112
2. Thai Chicken Salad, page 22
3. Greek Salad, page 56
4. Zuppa Fagioli, page 111

Props Courtesy Of: Artifacts, Le Gnome, The Bay

# BROTHY PASTA SOUP

*No work to this. Simple and tasty.*

| Condensed beef consommé | 10 oz. | 284 mL |
| Water | 1 cup | 250 mL |
| Ditali (small) pasta | 1 cup | 250 mL |
| Vegetable cocktail juice | 2 cups | 500 mL |

**Grated Parmesan cheese, sprinkle**

Combine consommé, water, pasta and cocktail juice in medium saucepan. Stir. Bring to a boil. Cover. Simmer for 10 minutes until pasta is tender.

Sprinkle Parmesan cheese over individual servings. Makes about 3¹⁄₂ cups (875 mL).

*1 cup (250 mL):* 142 Calories; 0.5 g Total Fat; 974 mg Sodium; 8 g Protein; 27 g Carbohydrate; 1 g Dietary Fiber

# MACARONI BROCCOLI SOUP

*Tomato juice and broccoli for eye-appealing color contrast.*

| Bacon slices, chopped | 2 | 2 |
| Tomato juice | 3 cups | 750 mL |
| Water | 5 cups | 1.25 L |
| Elbow macaroni | 2 cups | 500 mL |
| Broccoli florets | 1¹⁄₂ cups | 375 mL |
| Salt | 1 tsp. | 5 mL |
| Pepper | ¹⁄₄ tsp. | 1 mL |
| Garlic powder | ¹⁄₄ tsp. | 1 mL |
| Dried sweet basil | ¹⁄₄ tsp. | 1 mL |

**Grated Parmesan cheese, sprinkle**

Brown bacon in large pot or Dutch oven until cooked but not crisp. Drain.

Add next 8 ingredients. Bring to a boil. Cover. Simmer for about 10 minutes, stirring occasionally, until macaroni is tender.

Sprinkle individual servings with Parmesan cheese. Makes about 7 cups (1.75 L).

*1 cup (250 mL):* 152 Calories; 1.5 g Total Fat; 811 mg Sodium; 6 g Protein; 29 g Carbohydrate; 2 g Dietary Fiber

1. Tuna Bisque, page 104
2. Meatball Soup, page 74
3. Shelled Zucchini Soup, page 114
4. Asparagus Leek Soup, page 116

Props Courtesy Of: C C On Whyte, Stokes, The Bay

## ORZO MUSHROOM SOUP

*Orzo (OHR-zoh) in Italian means "barley." It is actually a tiny, rice-shaped pasta. Use a variety of mushrooms for more flavor.*

| | | |
|---|---|---|
| **Fresh mushrooms, finely chopped** | **1½ lbs.** | **680 g** |
| **All-purpose flour** | **3 tbsp.** | **50 mL** |
| **Garlic cloves, minced** | **3** | **3** |
| **Water** | **6 cups** | **1.5 L** |
| **Beef bouillon powder** | **3 tbsp.** | **50 mL** |
| **Green onions, thinly sliced** | **3** | **3** |
| **Salt** | **1 tsp.** | **5 mL** |
| **Freshly ground pepper** | **½-1 tsp.** | **2-5 mL** |
| **Uncooked orzo pasta** | **½ cup** | **125 mL** |
| **Non-fat sour cream** | **1 cup** | **250 mL** |

Heat lightly greased large pot or Dutch oven until hot. Sauté mushrooms, flour and garlic for 5 minutes.

Add water, bouillon powder, green onion, salt and pepper. Simmer for 15 minutes.

Add pasta. Simmer for 10 minutes. Remove from heat. Stir in sour cream. Makes 9 cups (2.25 L).

*1 cup (250 mL): 67 Calories; 0.8 g Total Fat: 911 mg Sodium; 4 g Protein; 22 g Carbohydrate; 1 g Dietary Fiber*

## TORTELLINI IN BROTH

*Very quick and easy to prepare.*

| | | |
|---|---|---|
| **Condensed chicken broth (10 oz., 284 mL, each)** | **3** | **3** |
| **Water** | **3½ cups** | **875 mL** |
| **Broccoli florets** | **2 cups** | **500 mL** |
| **Green onions, thinly sliced** | **4** | **4** |
| **Commercial cheese or meat-filled tortellini** | **1 lb.** | **454 g** |
| **Grated light Parmesan cheese, sprinkle (optional)** | | |

Combine chicken broth and water in large pot or Dutch oven. Bring to a boil.

Add broccoli, green onion and tortellini. Simmer, partially covered, for 4 to 5 minutes. Add tortellini. Bring to a boil. Cook, partially covered, for 10 to 12 minutes until tender but firm.

Sprinkle Parmesan cheese over individual servings. Makes 9 cups (2.25 L).

*1 cup (250 mL): 144 Calories; 2 g Total Fat; 913 mg Sodium; 10 g Protein; 22 g Carbohydrate; 1 g Dietary Fiber*

Pictured on front cover.

*For perfect pasta, cook in enough water for the pasta to move freely. The general rule is to use 4 to 6 quarts (4 to 6 L) water for 1 lb. (454 g) uncooked pasta.*

# ZUPPA FAGIOLI

*Fagioli (Faj-YOH-lee) is the Italian word for "beans." A hearty Italian meal-in-one bean soup. Only 20 minutes preparation time.*

| | | |
|---|---|---|
| Olive oil | 1 tsp. | 5 mL |
| Extra lean ground beef | ½ lb. | 225 g |
| Chopped onion | 1 cup | 250 mL |
| Chopped white celery heart (use inside ribs with leaves) | 1 cup | 250 mL |
| Medium carrot, grated | 1 | 1 |
| Large garlic clove, minced | 1 | 1 |
| Can of tomatoes, with juice, processed | 28 oz. | 796 mL |
| Can of white kidney beans, with liquid | 19 oz. | 540 mL |
| Can of beans in tomato sauce, with liquid | 14 oz. | 398 mL |
| Liquid beef bouillon concentrate | 2 tsp. | 10 mL |
| Tomato paste | 2 tbsp. | 30 mL |
| Dried sweet basil | 2 tsp. | 10 mL |
| Dried whole oregano | ¼ tsp. | 1 mL |
| Dried thyme | ¼ tsp. | 1 mL |
| Dried crushed chilies | ¼ tsp. | 1 mL |
| Salt | ½ tsp. | 2 mL |
| Pepper | ⅛ tsp. | 0.5 mL |
| Granulated sugar | ½ tsp. | 2 mL |
| Water | 3 cups | 750 mL |
| Uncooked tubetti (very small) pasta | 1 cup | 250 mL |
| Freshly ground pepper, sprinkle | | |

Heat olive oil in large pot or Dutch oven. Add next 5 ingredients. Scramble-fry until beef is browned and vegetables are tender-crisp. Drain.

Add next 12 ingredients. Stir well.

Add water. Stir. Cover. Bring to a boil. Reduce heat. Simmer for 1 hour.

Stir in pasta. Simmer for 10 to 15 minutes until pasta is cooked.

Grind pepper over individual servings. Makes 12 cups (3 L).

*1 cup (250 mL): 180 Calories; 3.8 g Total Fat; 660 mg Sodium; 11 g Protein; 27 g Carbohydrate; 7 g Dietary Fiber*

Pictured on page 107.

*To check for freshness of dried beans, tip them into a bowl of cold water, and discard any that float to the surface, since this is an indication of insect or mold damage.*

## NOODLES AND SOUP

*A thick and filling Chinese-style soup. Cook, cool and shred chicken the day before. Pour stock into large measure. Cover and chill both. Skim fat off stock in the morning. Prepare and cook mushrooms. Cover. Cook noodles ahead and keep in water.*

| | | |
|---|---|---|
| **Boneless, skinless chicken breast halves** | ½ **lb.** | **225 g** |
| **Water** | **2 cups** | **500 mL** |
| **Chinese dried mushrooms (see Note)** | **4** | **4** |
| **Water** | **1 cup** | **250 mL** |
| **Medium egg noodles** | **8 oz.** | **225 g** |
| **Boiling water** | **3 qts.** | **3 L** |
| **Cooking oil (optional)** | **1 tbsp.** | **15 mL** |
| **Salt** | **2 tsp.** | **10 mL** |
| **Reserved chicken stock, plus water to make** | **3 cups** | **750 mL** |
| **Frozen chopped spinach (10 oz., 300 g)** | ½ | ½ |
| **Green onions, cut into 1 inch (2.5 cm) lengths and slivered** | **2** | **2** |
| **Can of bamboo shoots (8 oz., 227 mL), drained and slivered** | ½ | ½ |
| **Sherry (or alcohol-free sherry)** | **2 tsp.** | **10 mL** |
| **Soy sauce** | **1 tbsp.** | **15 mL** |
| **Granulated sugar** | ½ **tsp.** | **2 mL** |
| **Ground ginger** | ¼ **tsp.** | **1 mL** |
| **Salt** | **1 tsp.** | **5 mL** |

Cook chicken in first amount of water in small saucepan for about 30 minutes until tender. Remove chicken, reserving stock. Cool chicken. Shred with fork.

Soak mushrooms in second amount of water in small bowl for 25 minutes. Remove. Squeeze dry. Discard water and hard stems. Sliver mushrooms.

Cook noodles in boiling water, cooking oil and first amount of salt in large uncovered pot or Dutch oven for 5 to 7 minutes until tender but firm. Drain. Rinse with cold water. Drain.

Measure remaining 9 ingredients into large saucepan. Add chicken, mushrooms and noodles. Cook for about 5 minutes to warm noodles. Makes about 6 cups (1.5 L).

*1 cup (250 mL): 221 Calories; 2.4 g Total Fat; 679 mg Sodium; 16 g Protein; 34 g Carbohydrate; 2 g Dietary Fiber*

Pictured on page 107.

**Note:** Substitute any type of fresh mushroom and omit second amount of water. The dried mushrooms have a stronger flavor than fresh mushrooms.

*If boneless chicken breasts are double the price as those with bone in, they are a good buy. The bones in chicken breasts are about half of the total weight so the price is about the same per serving.*

# Vegetable Soups

**V**egetables are an important part of our daily diet, but motivating fussy eaters to finish them can be a problem for many families. The solution is simple and right here in this impressive collection of recipes. Herbed Tomato Soup, page 117, features a blend of tomatoes and fresh herbs that will appeal to children and adults alike.

## SPLIT PEA SOUP

*Try this different version containing hot Italian sausage and potato.*

| | | |
|---|---|---|
| Water | 8 cups | 2 L |
| Dried green split peas | 2 cups | 500 mL |
| Hot Italian sausages | ½ lb. | 225 g |
| Diced potato | 1½ cups | 375 mL |
| Diced or sliced carrot | 1 cup | 250 mL |
| Chopped onion | 1 cup | 250 mL |
| Chopped celery | ½ cup | 125 mL |

Measure water and split peas into large pot or Dutch oven. Bring to a boil. Simmer, uncovered, stirring occasionally, for 1 hour.

Cook sausages in medium frying pan until well browned. Drain. Slice each sausage lengthwise into quarters. Cut into ¼ inch (6 mm) pieces. Add sausage pieces to pea mixture.

Add potato, carrot, onion and celery. Stir. Simmer, uncovered, stirring occasionally, for 40 minutes. Makes about 10 cups (2.5 L).

***1 cup (250 mL):*** *213 Calories; 3.3 g Total Fat; 116 mg Sodium; 14 g Protein; 34 g Carbohydrate; 7 g Dietary Fiber*

Pictured on front cover.

*To thicken soup, add 1 tbsp. (15 mL) or more of instant potato flakes.*

## SHELLED ZUCCHINI SOUP

*This is a colorful soup that is full of flavor.*

| | | |
|---|---|---|
| Mild Italian sausages, sliced ¼ inch (6 mm) thick | ½ lb. | 225 g |
| Chopped onion | 1 cup | 250 mL |
| Condensed chicken broth (10 oz., 284 mL, each) | 2 | 2 |
| Water | 3 cups | 750 mL |
| Garlic clove(s), minced | 1-2 | 1-2 |
| Coarsely grated zucchini, with peel | 4 cups | 1 L |
| Grated carrot | 1 cup | 250 mL |
| Italian seasoning | 1 tsp. | 5 mL |
| Dried sweet basil | ½ tsp. | 2 mL |
| Ground oregano | ½ tsp. | 2 mL |
| Granulated sugar | ½ tsp. | 2 mL |
| Uncooked tiny shell pasta | 1 cup | 250 mL |

Scramble-fry sausage and onion in large pot or Dutch oven until no pink remains in meat. Drain fat.

Add next 9 ingredients. Stir. Bring to a boil. Cover. Simmer slowly for 1 hour.

Add pasta. Stir. Simmer for about 10 minutes until pasta is tender. Add a bit more water if too thick. Makes 8 cups (2 L).

*1 cup (250 mL): 211 Calories; 11 g Total Fat; 759 mg Sodium; 11 g Protein; 17 g Carbohydrate; 3 g Dietary Fiber*

**Variation:** Top individual servings with mozzarella cheese slice and broil until cheese is melted and browned.

Pictured on page 108.

## VEGETABLE SOUP

*Chock full of vegetables. This freezes well.*

| | | |
|---|---|---|
| Diced or cubed potato | 2 cups | 500 mL |
| Chopped onion | 1 cup | 250 mL |
| Chopped cabbage, lightly packed | 1 cup | 250 mL |
| Thinly sliced carrot | ½ cup | 125 mL |
| Diced rutabaga (yellow turnip) | ¼ cup | 60 mL |
| Diced parsnip | ¼ cup | 60 mL |
| Water | 2 cups | 500 mL |
| Parsley flakes | 2 tsp. | 10 mL |
| Vegetable cocktail juice | 2 cups | 500 mL |
| Salt | 1 tsp. | 5 mL |
| Pepper | ¼ tsp. | 1 mL |

Combine first 8 ingredients in large saucepan. Bring to a boil. Cover. Simmer for about 30 minutes until vegetables are tender.

Add cocktail juice, salt and pepper. Stir. Heat through. Makes about 9 cups (2.25 L).

*1 cup (250 mL): 55 Calories; 0.2 g Total Fat; 519 mg Sodium; 2 g Protein; 13 g Carbohydrate; 1 g Dietary Fiber*

*Did someone extra show up for dinner? To make your soup go further, add an extra can of tomatoes, chopped fresh vegetables and/or some cooked pasta.*

# FRENCH ONION SOUP

*One of the best food treats in France. You will
need ovenproof bowls for this scrumptious soup.*

| | | |
|---|---|---|
| **Margarine** | 6 tbsp. | 100 mL |
| **Medium onions, thinly sliced (about 7)** | 2½ lbs. | 1.1 kg |
| **Granulated sugar** | 1 tbsp. | 15 mL |
| **All-purpose flour** | 2 tbsp. | 30 mL |
| **Salt** | ½ tsp. | 2 mL |
| **Pepper** | ¼ tsp. | 1 mL |
| **Beef bouillon cubes (⅕ oz., 6 g, each)** | 7 | 7 |
| **Boiling water** | 8 cups | 2 L |
| **French bread slices, toasted and cubed** | 8 | 8 |
| **Grated Gruyère cheese** | 2 cups | 500 mL |

Melt margarine in frying pan. Add onion and
sugar. Sauté slowly until medium brown in color,
stirring often.

Sprinkle with flour, salt and pepper. Stir. Cook for
5 minutes.

Dissolve bouillon cubes in boiling water in large
saucepan. Add contents of frying pan. Bring to a
boil. Simmer, covered, for 20 minutes.

Cover bottom of 8 individual bowls with toast
cubes. Divide soup over top. Place about ¼ cup
(60 mL) cheese over soup. Broil until cheese is
melted. Makes 10 cups (2.5 L).

*1 cup (250 mL): 256 Calories; 15.2 g Total Fat; 1365 mg
Sodium; 10 g Protein; 20 g Carbohydrate; 2 g Dietary Fiber*

# EGG FLOWER SOUP

*A soft looking soup. Not too filling before a meal.*

| | | |
|---|---|---|
| **Chicken bouillon cubes (⅕ oz., 6 g, each)** | 6 | 6 |
| **Boiling water** | 9 cups | 2.25 L |
| **Large eggs, fork-beaten** | 3 | 3 |
| **Cornstarch** | ⅓ cup | 75 mL |
| **Water** | ⅓ cup | 75 mL |
| **Salt** | ½ tsp. | 2 mL |
| **Pepper** | ⅛ tsp. | 0.5 mL |
| **Low-sodium soy sauce** | 1 tbsp. | 15 mL |
| **Thinly sliced green onion** | 1 tbsp. | 15 mL |

Dissolve bouillon cubes in boiling water in large
pot or Dutch oven.

Pour eggs slowly into boiling broth, stirring
continually, until eggs are cooked.

Mix next 5 ingredients in small bowl. Stir into
boiling broth until mixture is boiling and thickened.
Ladle soup into 8 individual bowls.

Garnish each serving with green onion. Makes
10 cups (2.5 L).

*1 cup (250 mL): 48 Calories; 1.7 g Total Fat; 1067 mg Sodium;
3 g Protein; 5 g Carbohydrate; trace Dietary Fiber*

Pictured on page 36.

## ASPARAGUS LEEK SOUP

*To save time, start chopping vegetables for the broth while chicken is poaching.*

| | | |
|---|---|---|
| Boneless, skinless chicken breast half | ¼ lb. | 113 g |
| White (or alcohol-free) wine | ¼ cup | 60 mL |
| Condensed chicken broth (10 oz., 284 mL, each) | 3 | 3 |
| Water | 4 cups | 1 L |
| Medium leek (white and tender green parts only) | 1 | 1 |
| Finely diced red or yellow pepper | ½ cup | 125 mL |
| Fresh asparagus, sliced into 1 inch (2.5 cm) lengths | 1 lb. | 454 g |
| Uncooked fusilli (spiral) pasta | 1 cup | 250 mL |
| Finely chopped fresh parsley (or 2 tsp., 10 mL, flakes) | 2 tbsp. | 30 mL |
| Pepper | ⅛ tsp. | 0.5 mL |

Place chicken breast and wine in small non-stick frying pan. Cover. Cook chicken for 3 to 4 minutes on each side. Remove lid. Cook until liquid is evaporated and chicken is browned on both sides. Remove chicken to cutting board. Cut into slivers.

Combine chicken broth and water in large pot or Dutch oven. Ladle a bit of broth into same frying pan used to cook chicken. Pour all browned flavoring back into broth in pot. This adds great flavor to soup.

Thinly slice leek crosswise. Add to broth. Stir. Add red pepper. Stir. Bring mixture to a boil. Simmer, partially covered, for 20 minutes.

Add asparagus, pasta and chicken. Stir. Cook for 12 to 15 minutes, partially covered, until asparagus and pasta are tender.

Stir in parsley and pepper. Makes 9 cups (2.25 L).

*1 cup (250 mL): 108 Calories; 1.5 g Total Fat; 642 mg Sodium; 10 g Protein; 12 g Carbohydrate; 2 g Dietary Fiber*

Pictured on page 108.

## TOMATO CABBAGE SOUP

*A full-bodied soup.*

| | | |
|---|---|---|
| Can of diced tomatoes, with juice | 19 oz. | 540 mL |
| Grated cabbage, lightly packed | 2 cups | 500 mL |
| Chopped onion | ½ cup | 125 mL |
| Packets low-sodium beef bouillon powder (¼ oz., 6.5 g, each) | 2 | 2 |
| Boiling water | 1 cup | 250 mL |
| Liquid sweetener | ¼ tsp. | 1 mL |
| Peas (fresh or frozen) | ¼ cup | 60 mL |

Pour tomatoes with juice into medium saucepan. Add cabbage and onion. Stir.

Dissolve bouillon powder in boiling water in cup. Add to saucepan. Stir. Bring to a boil. Cover. Simmer for about 20 minutes until vegetables are tender.

Add liquid sweetener and peas. Stir. Simmer for 3 to 4 minutes until peas are cooked. Makes 4 cups (1 L).

*1 cup (250 mL): 60 Calories; 0.9 g Total Fat; 531 mg Sodium; 3 g Protein; 12 g Carbohydrate; 3 g Dietary Fiber*

# HERBED TOMATO SOUP

*Rich red color. Lots of delicious tomato chunks.*
*Only ten minutes preparation time.*

| | | |
|---|---|---|
| Finely chopped onion | ½ cup | 125 mL |
| Garlic cloves, minced | 2 | 2 |
| Olive oil | 1 tsp. | 5 mL |
| Fennel seed | ½ tsp. | 2 mL |
| Ripe medium roma (plum) tomatoes, diced | 3 | 3 |
| Can of crushed tomatoes, with juice | 28 oz. | 796 mL |
| Condensed chicken broth | 10 oz. | 284 mL |
| Water | 1½ cups | 375 mL |
| Minced fresh sweet basil (or 1 tsp., 5 mL, dried) | 1 tbsp. | 15 mL |
| Minced fresh marjoram leaves (or ½ tsp., 2 mL, ground) | 1½ tsp. | 7 mL |
| Minced fresh oregano leaves (or ¼ tsp., 1 mL, ground) | 1 tsp. | 5 mL |
| Granulated sugar | ½ tsp. | 2 mL |
| Uncooked orzo (very small) pasta | ⅔ cup | 150 mL |
| Grated light Parmesan cheese product, sprinkle (optional) | | |
| Freshly ground pepper, sprinkle (optional) | | |

Sauté onion and garlic in olive oil in large non-stick frying pan until onion is soft. Add fennel seed. Sauté for 1 minute.

Add next 8 ingredients. Stir. Cover. Simmer for 30 to 40 minutes.

Add pasta. Simmer, uncovered, for 10 to 12 minutes, stirring occasionally, until pasta is tender but firm.

Sprinkle with Parmesan cheese and pepper. Makes 7 cups (1.75 L).

***1 cup (250 mL):*** *150 Calories; 2 g Total Fat; 465 mg Sodium; 7 g Protein; 27 g Carbohydrate; 3 g Dietary Fiber*

*To easily peel a garlic clove, place clove on a cutting board. Cover the clove with the flat side of a chef's knife blade, then firmly press down on the blade with your fist. This loosens the skin so that it comes right off.*

# GARLIC AND ONION SOUP

*This soup is best served the same day.
Preparation time is only 20 minutes.*

| | | |
|---|---|---|
| Olive oil | 1 tbsp. | 15 mL |
| Large onion, very thinly sliced then slivered | 1 | 1 |
| Garlic cloves, minced | 8 | 8 |
| Apple juice | 3 tbsp. | 50 mL |
| All-purpose flour | 1 tbsp. | 15 mL |
| White (or alcohol-free) wine | 1/2 cup | 125 mL |
| Water | 7 cups | 1.75 L |
| Beef bouillon powder | 2 tsp. | 10 mL |
| Bay leaves | 2 | 2 |
| Hot pepper sauce, dash | | |
| Chopped fresh parsley | 2 tbsp. | 30 mL |
| Salt | 2 tsp. | 10 mL |
| Pepper | 1/8 tsp. | 0.5 mL |
| Uncooked tri-colored fusilli (spiral) pasta | 1 1/2 cups | 375 mL |
| Liquid gravy browner | 1 1/2 tsp. | 7 mL |

Heat olive oil in medium non-stick frying pan. Sauté onion and garlic for 5 minutes. Add apple juice. Cover. Cook, stirring occasionally, until onion is very soft and golden.

Sprinkle with flour. Mix well. Transfer to large pot or Dutch oven. Stir in wine. Add next 7 ingredients. Bring to a boil.

Add pasta. Simmer for 10 to 15 minutes until pasta is tender. Stir in gravy browner. Makes 7 cups (1.75 L).

*1 cup (250 mL): 123 Calories; 2.4 g Total Fat; 1046 mg Sodium; 3 g Protein; 19 g Carbohydrate; 1 g Dietary Fiber*

# BORSCHT

*Lighter red than most. Lots of vegetables.*

| | | |
|---|---|---|
| Reserved beet juice | | |
| Packets low-sodium beef bouillon powder (1/4 oz., 6.5 g, each) | 2 | 2 |
| Boiling water | 3 1/2 cups | 875 mL |
| Coarsely grated cabbage, lightly packed | 2 cups | 500 mL |
| Chopped onion | 1 cup | 250 mL |
| Thinly sliced carrot | 1 cup | 250 mL |
| Ground cloves | 1/8 tsp. | 0.5 mL |
| Dill weed | 1/8 tsp. | 0.5 mL |
| Pepper | 1/8 tsp. | 0.5 mL |
| Can of diced beets, drained and juice reserved | 14 oz. | 398 mL |
| Low-fat plain yogurt | 4 tbsp. | 60 mL |

Put reserved beet juice into medium saucepan. Bring to a boil. Add bouillon powder and boiling water. Stir to dissolve.

Add next 6 ingredients. Stir. Bring to a boil. Cover. Simmer for about 25 minutes until carrot is tender.

Add beets. Return to boiling just until beets are heated.

Serve with dollop of yogurt on top. Makes about 6 1/2 cups (1.6 L).

*1 cup (250 mL): 48 Calories; trace Total Fat; 342 mg Sodium; 2 g Protein; 10 g Carbohydrate; 2 g Dietary Fiber*

# measurement tables

Throughout this book measurements are given in Conventional and Metric measure. To compensate for differences between the two measurements due to rounding, a full metric measure is not always used. The cup used is the standard 8 fluid ounce. Temperature is given in degrees Fahrenheit and Celsius. Baking pan measurements are in inches and centimetres as well as quarts and litres. An exact metric conversion is given below as well as the working equivalent (Standard Measure).

## OVEN TEMPERATURES

| Fahrenheit (°F) | Celsius (°C) |
|---|---|
| 175° | 80° |
| 200° | 95° |
| 225° | 110° |
| 250° | 120° |
| 275° | 140° |
| 300° | 150° |
| 325° | 160° |
| 350° | 175° |
| 375° | 190° |
| 400° | 205° |
| 425° | 220° |
| 450° | 230° |
| 475° | 240° |
| 500° | 260° |

## SPOONS

| Conventional Measure | Metric Exact Conversion Millilitre (mL) | Metric Standard Measure Millilitre (mL) |
|---|---|---|
| 1/8 teaspoon (tsp.) | 0.6 mL | 0.5 mL |
| 1/4 teaspoon (tsp.) | 1.2 mL | 1 mL |
| 1/2 teaspoon (tsp.) | 2.4 mL | 2 mL |
| 1 teaspoon (tsp.) | 4.7 mL | 5 mL |
| 2 teaspoons (tsp.) | 9.4 mL | 10 mL |
| 1 tablespoon (tbsp.) | 14.2 mL | 15 mL |

## CUPS

| Conventional Measure | Metric Exact Conversion Millilitre (mL) | Metric Standard Measure Millilitre (mL) |
|---|---|---|
| 1/4 cup (4 tbsp.) | 56.8 mL | 60 mL |
| 1/3 cup (5 1/3 tbsp.) | 75.6 mL | 75 mL |
| 1/2 cup (8 tbsp.) | 113.7 mL | 125 mL |
| 2/3 cup (10 2/3 tbsp.) | 151.2 mL | 150 mL |
| 3/4 cup (12 tbsp.) | 170.5 mL | 175 ml |
| 1 cup (16 tbsp.) | 227.3 mL | 250 mL |
| 4 1/2 cups | 1022.9 mL | 1000 mL (1 L) |

## PANS

| Conventional Inches | Metric Centimetres |
|---|---|
| 8x8 inch | 20x20 cm |
| 9x9 inch | 22x22 cm |
| 9x13 inch | 22x33 cm |
| 10x15 inch | 25x38 cm |
| 11x17 inch | 28x43 cm |
| 8x2 inch round | 20x5 cm |
| 9x2 inch round | 22x5 cm |
| 10x4 1/2 inch tube | 25x11 cm |
| 8x4x3 inch loaf | 20x10x7.5 cm |
| 9x5x3 inch loaf | 22x12.5x7.5 cm |

## DRY MEASUREMENTS

| Conventional Measure Ounces (oz.) | Metric Exact Conversion Grams (g) | Metric Standard Measure Grams (g) |
|---|---|---|
| 1 oz. | 28.3 g | 28 g |
| 2 oz. | 56.7 g | 57 g |
| 3 oz. | 85.0 g | 85 g |
| 4 oz. | 113.4 g | 125 g |
| 5 oz. | 141.7 g | 140 g |
| 6 oz. | 170.1 g | 170 g |
| 7 oz. | 198.4 g | 200 g |
| 8 oz. | 226.8 g | 250 g |
| 16 oz. | 453.6 g | 500 g |
| 32 oz. | 907.2 g | 1000 g (1 kg) |

## CASSEROLES (CANADA & BRITAIN)

| Standard Size Casserole | Exact Metric Measure |
|---|---|
| 1 qt. (5 cups) | 1.13 L |
| 1 1/2 qts. (7 1/2 cups) | 1.69 L |
| 2 qts. (10 cups) | 2.25 L |
| 2 1/2 qts. (12 1/2 cups) | 2.81 L |
| 3 qts. (15 cups) | 3.38 L |
| 4 qts. (20 cups) | 4.5 L |
| 5 qts. (25 cups) | 5.63 L |

## CASSEROLES (UNITED STATES)

| Standard Size Casserole | Exact Metric Measure |
|---|---|
| 1 qt. (4 cups) | 900 mL |
| 1 1/2 qts. (6 cups) | 1.35 L |
| 2 qts. (8 cups) | 1.8 L |
| 2 1/2 qts. (10 cups) | 2.25 L |
| 3 qts. (12 cups) | 2.7 L |
| 4 qts. (16 cups) | 3.6 L |
| 5 qts. (20 cups) | 4.5 L |

# index

**121**